fresh wood

Foreword: Conversations with
Sam Maloof On Student Design

new designers v.1

By Greg Asbury and Corinne Cortinas

M tra
PUBLISHING GROUP
Sierra Madre, California

Fresh Wood: New Designers Vol. 1

first printing

Principal editing and photography by Greg Asbury.

Design and layout by Corinne Cortinas
Cover photo by Joseph Byrd & Associates Inc.
Additional photos by Smith Asbury, Inc.
Ashley Nichole Hilton photos by Seth Tice Lewis
Donated photos from Brittany Davis, John Donley, John VanErem, Matthew Gardner, Andrew Housley, Jon Plummer, Justin Porcano, Remington Ryan Wither, Katie Richardson, Brian Sanderson, Drew Soderborg, and Jason Tippetts.

Published by Mitra Publishing Group

225 North Lima Street, Suite 6

Sierra Madre, California 91024

United States of America

ISBN: 0-9654003-3-6

Printed in China by Palace Press International

With contributions
and editing by
Judy Smith
Nancy Fister
Margrit Lehmann

On Student Design

Outside it was a hot hazy August afternoon in Southern California. Across the street at Disneyland, the happiest place on Earth was packed with vacationing families. But inside the cavernous Anaheim Convention Center things were buzzing — literally. It was the Association of Woodworking and Furnishings Suppliers® Fair. This biennial gathering of the industry fills the enormous glass and steel convention halls to capacity with the latest in woodworking and furniture equipment, machinery and hardware. Over four days, more than 20,000 people attend this show which is a must see for professionals in the woodworking, cabinet, and furnishings industries.

I was walking across the acres of terrazzo in the lobby towards the AWFS®Fair Student Design Exhibit in step with Sam Maloof, and a small entourage consisting of his current wife Beverly, his valiant manager Rosyln Bock and Sam's dedicated assistants — "The Boys" — David Wade, Mike Johnson, and Larry White who have collectively worked in his shop for nearly sixty years.

About seven years ago, the organizers of the AWFS®Fair were inspired to create a national student design contest inviting the best and brightest upcoming furniture designers to submit their works for judging and display at the Fair. It was hoped that the competition would showcase new work and provide a forum for elegant design. This year, there were over 50 finalists from high schools and universities in a tour de force of woodworking skill and craftsmanship. Hopeful entries had been received from all over the U.S. and Canada.

Sam was at the 2003 Fair in order to present the Best of Show Award to the winning entry in the Student Design competition later this evening. This is a stunning trophy that he created from one of his characteristic walnut chair arms. A small piece of an actual Maloof — for any woodworker, that was to die for!

Sam Maloof is arguably the finest contemporary woodworker and furniture designer in our country. He has left an impression on aspiring woodworkers and studio furniture designers for the last 60 years. Sam is unique among master craftsmen. His work is in the Smithsonian, the White House, and has appeared at the Vatican. In 1985, Sam received the John D. and Catherine T. MacArthur Foundation Award. Previously, the "genius" award had been the exclusive province of scholars scientists, and authors.

Maloof's house and workshops have been enshrined as an Historic Landmark. Former President Jimmy Carter owns several of his works, as do celebrities and luminaries. But Sam's story is a chapter from Horatio Alger — one of nine siblings in an immigrant family from Lebanon struggling to make it in pre-depression America. Sam was a gifted graphic designer before World War II; working first for an industrial manufacturer and then for Millard Sheets, one of America's preeminent painters. He made a precipitous career switch to woodworking in 1949. His first wife Alfreda Ward Maloof was "the heart and soul of my whole life and work." It was her unwavering support that allowed Sam to realize his craft. Although she passed away in late 1998, today Sam still wistfully refers to Freda as though she just stepped out of the room to get a cup of tea. Indeed she never seems far from the heart and soul of this remarkable artist.

He credits Freda, Beverly, Roz, and the Boys — those that have worked devotedly in his shop for much of his success. There seems to be a lesson in his orbit; truly great visionaries need to have not just tremendous faith in themselves but also a like measure of

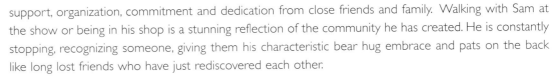

Conversations with Sam Maloof

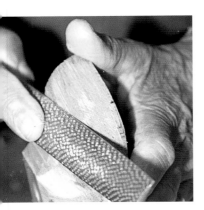

support, organization, commitment and dedication from close friends and family. Walking with Sam at the show or being in his shop is a stunning reflection of the community he has created. He is constantly stopping, recognizing someone, giving them his characteristic bear hug embrace and pats on the back like long lost friends who have just rediscovered each other.

Sam, who is now 87, walked strong and purposefully through the lobby in Anaheim, stopping to chat with everyone who recognized his slight bespectacled form. Not only is Sam Maloof one of the greatest living masters of the art, he is also one of the kindest, and most accessible. Following Sam is like being carried along in a vortex. You know that you are in the presence of someone with special gifts. And yet he is not the least bit pretentious. Always willing to stop and reminisce, or offer a helpful tip, he is the ultimate mentor.

Sam is never far from his roots or the memories of tough beginnings as a designer, "I've been very fortunate to be able to sell furniture. This year at the AWFS®Fair they had some of the nicest things I've seen." How important is a design competition to aspiring designers? Sam offered his own experience, "I happened to win a national poster contest, and it really started me out. I was going to a little high school in Chino — there were only about 15 kids in my class. The teacher had never taught art in her life before so she let me do whatever I wanted. That got me going and then I went into architecture and mechanical engineering drawing." It was the contest that got the attention of Walt Disney and others who tried to entice him with job offers while still in high school.

Seventy years later, Kyle MacMillan, student design finalist from Pittsburg State University, echoed these same thoughts with a new twist, "I was just sitting around drawing on the computer... it started with a vision and then I drew it out in AutoCAD. From that I knew what I had to do, I just needed to figure out how to do it. And so I entered the contest."

Maloof agreed, "You know, so much of design is computerized now. I mean if you don't know how to work with computers you get nowhere."

At the Student Design Exhibit, Sam sauntered past the pieces displayed with their presentation boards ranging from hand drawn concepts to rendered components ready for CNC milling. He asked whether I knew who the winner of his trophy was. The judging had been completed the previous evening by five well-respected industry experts. I nodded and was about to say whom when he cut me off, "Let's see if I can pick out the winner, don't tell me," he winked back in my direction. Methodically, Sam reviewed the entries with an appraising eye. There were several entries attributed to Maloof by students. Two rockers and a table all carefully reproduced and reinterpreted with the student's own flourishes. Maloof was not drawn to his own reflective pieces. Asked whether he minded that others try to imitate his work, Sam mused, "I don't mind, I still know which ones are mine." Eugene Morgan, who put in over 600 hours on his Maloof inspired rocker agreed, "If I'm about a quarter as good as Sam then I'd be pretty happy."

Indeed there are very few who can approach the level of his work. For Sam it is not just about design but it is also about function and comfort, "It doesn't matter how beautiful it looks, how well finished, if it doesn't sit well, then it's a lousy chair."

Stopping to inspect a table or chair, offering gentle advice to aspiring woodworkers, "That table would be a little more balanced if you'd make the legs a little wider," he offered a young high school woodworker from Portland, Oregon, whose walnut drop-leaf table had been copied from a Maloof design. "But that table is pretty good."

After several circuits around the exhibit, Sam was drawn back to a reclining chaise that seemed to have minimalist form within ergonomic curves. It was made of bent wood plies sandwiched between two metal layers. Held together by rivets, the outer metal layer pinned an array of foam balls covered in shiny blue elastic fabric to its face. This formed a bed of foam nuggets in a clean elegant swoosh. The whole recliner was balanced on thin curved aluminum legs.

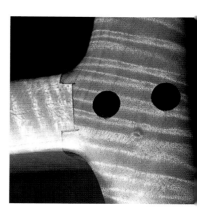

"I think this is my pick", Sam offered reclining on the chaise. Sure enough, it was the unanimous choice of the judges. But the judging wasn't that easy. As A.J. Hamler offered before the final judging, "...when it came time to decide which pieces should be finalists...I gave my recommendation to far more of the pieces than event organizers anticipated."[1]

Later in the evening, Sam presented his trophy to a beaming Ryan Wither from Savannah College of Art and Design. Thinking there was some hidden detail, some magic calculated compound curve or the way the arm table nested with the chaise, I asked him why he liked this piece so much. Sam said simply, "Well when I laid down on it I didn't want to get up again..."

And then I understood. Sam Maloof reduces form and function to the most elemental dance. Part of the magic of Sam Maloof's work is in how he is able to match his sculptural forms with precise balance and comfort. In the signature compound curves, delicate spindles, book matched grain, fiddle back maple, or pinned joints, it's true he is releasing the character of the wood. But beyond that, what Sam Maloof creates in his pieces that eludes his imitators is function and comfort at an unexpected level. Sit on one of his rockers, lift your legs off the ground and you are perfectly balanced, the chair does not move. That is the perfection that Sam saw in this piece and what he was coaching others to achieve. "I liked that boy. His work was really good. I'll bet if I was a manufacturer I'd pick that up right away."

Shortly after the AWFS®Fair, Corinne Cortinas and I went up to his shop to visit with Sam further about students and designers who are starting out today. The trip up to the Sam and Alfreda Maloof Foundation campus is exhilarating. Vineyards and orange groves once flourished on this alluvial fan washing out from the base of the San Gabriel Mountains. They are almost completely gone now, replaced by stuccoed tract houses as commuters stretch out along the freeway. It isn't difficult to imagine the early California days when Sam Maloof and his wife Freda created an oasis of art. A fragmentary arts colony existed in this rough and tumble Inland Valley far from the ocean breezes of Los Angeles and its frenzied sprawl. In 2001, Sam's original house and workshops were all moved lock stock and bandsaw from the old location in the path of Southern California's latest freeway up the hill to Carnelian Drive in Alta Loma.

Today, all of the buildings have been reassembled and restored forming a unique campus that enshrines a museum and preserves Sam's working spaces just as they always were. Looking out over the sweeping Pomona Valley, it is a short distance from where Sam Maloof started his career and yet it's a world apart. Sam still works 10 to 12 hours a day in his own shop. He and his assistants produce about fifty pieces a year, leaving him with backorders well into his centenarian years.

1.   A.J. Hamler, "I've Seen the Future and It Is Good," *Woodshop News*, August 2003.

Conversations with Sam Maloof

I walked into Sam's private shop through the sanding room, past great slabs of walnut, over clamps scattered in racks and strewn on the concrete floor, around skeletons of half assembled chairs with corner posts and legs sticking up from the shaved and cupped seats like so many ribs. Hunched over a huge 20 inch bandsaw in front of me was Sam, dust covered, squinting through his thick glasses, feeding a rough slab of walnut through the blade. He ripped through the wood like butter turning it into the curved winglet of an arm. Masterfully, he used the bandsaw without a fence or guide to pare away extra material until he was satisfied with the rough three dimensional form. "I don't usually let people watch me", Sam glanced backwards. "Sorry to bother you," I said timidly realizing my faux-pas.

"That's OK, I knew you were coming." He grinned impishly.

In case you think this is simply a production line, no piece is untouched by Sam. In fact, the precision with how he works is uncanny. Sam is able to slice out mirror matching compound curved chair arms in a few minutes on a bandsaw, freehand. He takes the bandsawn form, ratchets it into a bench vise and in the space of about fifteen minutes he transforms it into a fluid form in wood using only his Surform™ and rasp. Iconically, he smoothes and shapes only by eye and touch. His hands continuously stroke the piece, feeling for high spots or a curve that doesn't quite conform. There are no rulers or tapes in evidence.

"One day I had about eight chairs that were about finished and a fellow was looking them over. He said, 'You don't use calipers or any measuring devices.' I said I just use my thumb and forefinger (holding them slightly apart and squinting through the gap). He asked how accurate that was and I guessed about a quarter of an inch. So I was thinking those chairs might be off by about that much. He left and went into the house. At lunchtime he came back out and said, 'Sam you're all wrong! I measured the chairs.' I thought, OK maybe it was three eighths of an inch. He exclaimed, 'It's right on the button! That's how I do everything – I eyeball it.'"

We had come to Sam's shop after the AWFS®Fair to review the entries and reflect on his views about design in the contemporary market. Designers and woodworkers face a market in which craft has fled across the Pacific, hollowing out mainstream furniture manufacturing in the U.S. I asked Sam what he thought of the current pressures to make furniture by all manner of machinery and from areas where labor was so low as to make it impossible to compete head-on with traditional shops in the U.S.

"From China, they're putting manufacturers out of business. They can ship over here cheaply. I have a friend who owns about a million square feet of warehouse. They're building another one now. The stuff comes in so fast and dozens of semi-trailers come through to take it to WalMart, COSTCO, Target-stores like that, and that puts the small manufacturer out of business. They can make more in a day than I made in my life. The stuff I do is old hat!"

Indeed this is a problem that most manufacturers are staring at in the U.S. And it's not clear what future awaits the next generation of designers and woodworkers. I asked Sam about how he was able to stay true to his art.

"I had a show in the Armory in New York City many years ago. Mr. Morgenthal took to me. They wanted to buy the three pieces I had there to manufacture in production. They were going to make these en masse. I didn't want to do that. About a year later, I was on the board of the Crafts Council of New

York and a fellow I knew came up to me. He was an attorney and he said 'Sam why did you turn us down?' I didn't know what he was talking about. 'My company, RayMor, offered you $22 million for those three pieces and you wouldn't sell them. Why?' I said, 'because I didn't want to prostitute myself and that was it. The integrity meant more than money.''

Sam lived that belief resolutely. Until he received the MacArthur grant in 1985 with its $375,000 stipend, he and Freda did not have financial security. Integrity and being true to your art are important values that today's students need to integrate into the fast-paced global markets that they are drawn into competition with. Sam acknowledged those difficulties but also provided some insight into the core values that sustained him. I wondered, "What kept you going back when you worked for Millard Sheets and did woodwork on the side? Somehow you must have had an idea that you were going to succeed?''

"No ifs ands or buts it was Freda. We lived on a shoestring. I was the one who thought I should go back to drafting — she was the heart and soul — still is. It took me about 40 years and Freda was very careful about finances, then it took off. I can still see her at the sink washing dishes. I walked in and said 'Freda, have a look at these.' I handed her two blue slips that were rejection notices. I thought she'd drop the dish and hug me saying, 'They don't know what they're doing!' But she took a towel and went back to washing dishes, 'Sam, rejection is good for you.' Those were the best words that I ever heard. Really.''

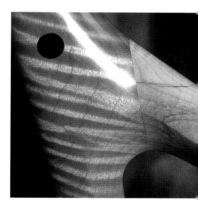

Lunchtime was approaching and there was now a shop full of friends who had dropped in. An accomplished woodworker who specialized in unique bowl turning. Sam's former pastor Gary Keene and his wife, Karen a spectacular fine arts painter. The phone was ringing constantly. Sam went to the wall phone in his shop answering calls himself just as he always does — another friend from Australia, a neighbor to report that his two dogs had gotten out and were down the road, the Anderson Ranch calling about next week's seminar. Despite all of the interruptions and diversions, he kept a laser focus on the question about what would he tell new designers and it just came down to this — "It's about the work. Try it. You just don't know until you do. You have to reach and also be true to your own integrity. Above all else something might be beautifully crafted but it just doesn't matter unless it sits well.''

With that he climbed into his Porsche and drove off to his favorite taco stand for lunch. Karen sat beside him, her red hair blowing; the silver roadster left a dust cloud billowing behind. Sam Maloof is an uncommon inspiration.

Contents

"I've seen the future – and it is good"

"I've just completed the most difficult woodworking project I've ever undertaken. And never touched a piece of wood in the process.

The project started several months ago when I was asked by the Association of Woodworking & Furnishings Suppliers® to be a judge for Student Design 2003.

Poring over this year's entries, I realized that selecting the best from among them wasn't the clear-cut task I had imagined. I went through the entries one-by-one, and marked my scores accordingly. Fortunately, I used pencil instead of ink, as I had to go back more times than I can remember to alter scores up and down as the full scope of the entries slowly unfolded.

Most of the scores I gave were quite high, and when it came time to decide which pieces should be finalists and shipped to California for final judging at the AWFS® Fair, I'm afraid I gave my recommendation to far more of the pieces than event organizers anticipated.

But the work of these students was so good, I could do little else. Add to that the fact that most of them were far less than half my age – many younger than my own student-age daughter – and their achievements are all the more remarkable.

We've learned from the many shops we've profiled in Woodshop News that finding skilled, motivated workers is often the most difficult part of running a successful woodworking business. Those of you in this situation will be happy to know that an eager crop of available talent is ripening all over the country.

On the other hand, those of you who fear talented competition had better get ready.

These kids are coming your way."

—A.J. Hamler
Editor, Woodshop News
"Used with permission of Woodshop News."

The Student Design Competition

**July 31-August 3, 2003
Anaheim, California**

The Association of Woodworking & Furnishings Suppliers® (AWFS®) is the largest national trade association in the United States representing companies that supply the home and commercial furnishings industry.

One of the Association's key goals is to encourage woodworking education and foster the links between industry and educational organizations. As part of this initiative, AWFS® launched the Student Design Contest in 1996.

The contest takes place biennially, to correspond with the Association's large trade event, the AWFS®Fair, taking place in the odd-numbered years in Anaheim, California. Contest finalists are prominently displayed at the event.

The contest is open to students who are enrolled in accredited high school and postsecondary schools in the United States and Canada. Students submit a range of work that encompasses innovative, traditional and manufacturable furniture projects. Students may submit more than one entry. All projects have to have been designed and/or built in a specified timeframe leading up to the Fair. (For 2003, the dates were September 1, 2002 through June 30, 2003.) A panel of judges reviews the entries and selects a group of finalists. High school and postsecondary entries are judged separately. Projects of the finalists are then shipped (by AWFS®) to the AWFS®Fair for display and final judging.

Projects may be entered in either a traditional or creative style group broken down into categories of Chairs, Tables, Casework/Cabinets, Upholstered Furniture and a Special Theme, chosen for each contest year. (The 2003 Special Theme was "Office Furniture of the Future"). First prizes and honorable mentions are given in each style and category, at both the high school and postsecondary levels. In addition a Best of Show Award and a People's Choice Award are given.

3

Judges

Andrew Glasgow, Executive Director – The Furniture Society

Andrew Glasgow is currently Executive Director of The Furniture Society, an international organization primarily serving studio furniture makers.

Glasgow has spent over 15 years in curatorial and administrative aspects of contemporary American craft, following four years in museum work on historical decorative arts of the Deep South. He has published numerous articles in arts and antiques publications.

Founded in 1997, the Furniture Society is a non-profit educational organization for and about studio furniture makers. The society involves educators, collectors, historians and gallery owners, as well as the makers of the furniture. The society seeks to advance the art of furniture making by inspiring creativity, promoting excellence and fostering an understanding of this art and its place in society.

A.J. Hamler, Editor – Woodshop News

A.J. Hamler is editor of *Woodshop News*, a monthly publication targeted to professional cabinetmakers, millwork shops and custom furniture makers.

A serious amateur woodworker himself, when he's not editing or writing for the magazine he'll most likely be in his workshop building a clock or a piece of furniture of his own design.

Hamler came to *Woodshop News* in 1997 following 25 years as a radio broadcaster (you can still hear him on-the-air from time to time in the greater Hartford, Connecticut, area). His writing efforts are not restricted to woodworking – Hamler has published two science fiction novels and several short stories, as well as numerous nonfiction articles on a variety of subjects ranging from astronomy to public speaking.

Sandor Nagyszalanczy – Designer/Craftsman

Born in Budapest, Hungary, Sandor Nagyszalanczy is a noted author, photographer, furniture designer and tool expert, whose background includes work in metal sculpture and high end custom cabinet making. His work has been shown in numerous galleries and is part of the permanent collection of the Minneapolis Institute of Art. Nagyszalanczy is a former senior editor of *Fine Woodworking* magazine, West Coast Editor of *American Woodworker*, and an editor of Taunton Press' Design Book Series, numbers 4, 5 and 6. He is the author and photographer of ten books on various woodworking and tool related topics, including *The Art of Fine Tools* and *The Homeowner's Ultimate Tool Guide*. He has written for numerous magazines, including *Cabinetmaker* and *Woodshop News* and is a frequent contributor to *Woodworker's Journal*. Nagyszalanczy has appeared in programs on the History Channel, ABC Television, and Home and Garden Television.

Beverly Namnoun, Corporate Account Manager
Herman Miller Workplace Resources

Beverly Namnoun works as a strategic partner with large organizations who are clients of the Herman Miller Workplace Resources, a Herman Miller dealership in the Southern California area. Herman Miller is one of the leading office furniture companies in the design, manufacture and distribution of furnishings, interior products and related services.

Beverly Namnoun began her career in the office furniture industry in 1980. Originally involved in educational sales on the east coast, she found her calling in the furniture industry and joined a Herman Miller dealership in Hartford, Connecticut. She later moved to Texas and then to California to work for Steelcase, another major office furniture manufacturer. In 1993, she joined Herman Miller Workplace Resources in California.

Alan Jay Paull, President – Taylor Desk Company

Alan Jay Paull grew up in the furniture making industry, and while his professional career spans 30 years, he jokes that he actually started when he was two years old. His family had owned and operated Paull Contract since 1923. He joined the family business at age 21 and took over the helm when his father retired two years later. In 1986, Paull Contract was acquired by the Taylor Chair Company, the oldest furniture manufacturing company in the country. Paull continues as president of the Taylor Desk Company.

Paull studied design and architecture at the Art Center College of Design. As president of Taylor Desk, he designs and engineers much of the office furniture. He was active for over five years with the Institute of Business Designers (IBD).

The Taylor Companies have earned an excellent reputation for designing and crafting fine office furniture that reflects progressive design and possesses marked quality. Production lines and custom furnishings are sold in showrooms throughout the USA.

2003 Student Design Contest Committee:

Duane Griffiths, Stiles Machinery, Committee Chair

Larry Hilchie, Weinig Group America

Joan Kemp, JK Enterprises

Jeff Oliverson, Mountain View Machinery

Tom Orlando, CTD Machines, Inc.

Best of Show

Remington Ryan Wither

The panel of five judges padded carefully around each entry in the exhibit hall. Each judge paused to look at details, turn over pieces, pull out drawers, stroke the glassy finishes. They focused critical eyes like a Hollywood director framing the scene, visualizing the aesthetic forms. After several hours, they had reviewed every remarkable piece in the exhibit and were tabulating their scores.

These were difficult decisions. The quality of work was extraordinary; contenders for the Best of Show Award cut across high school and postsecondary school programs. Some of the best design schools in the country had entered the competition and entries in the hunt included high school students whose work contended in this elite group. But there was one design that emerged above the others.

RELAXATION – a quirky but elegant design captured the Best of Show Award. Remington "Ryan" Wither, a graduate student at Savannah School of Design, created this stunning work in metal, fabric and wood as part of his Master of Fine Arts thesis. This is the fifth piece in a series that he created to respond to organization.

"This is the mental part of organization. It's intended for the user to come home at night and offer a spot of invulnerable retreat to regroup and contemplate."

When Sam Maloof presented the Best of Show Award to Ryan he remarked, "This is a really nice piece. When I laid down in it, I didn't want to get up again. That's good design."

Best of Show

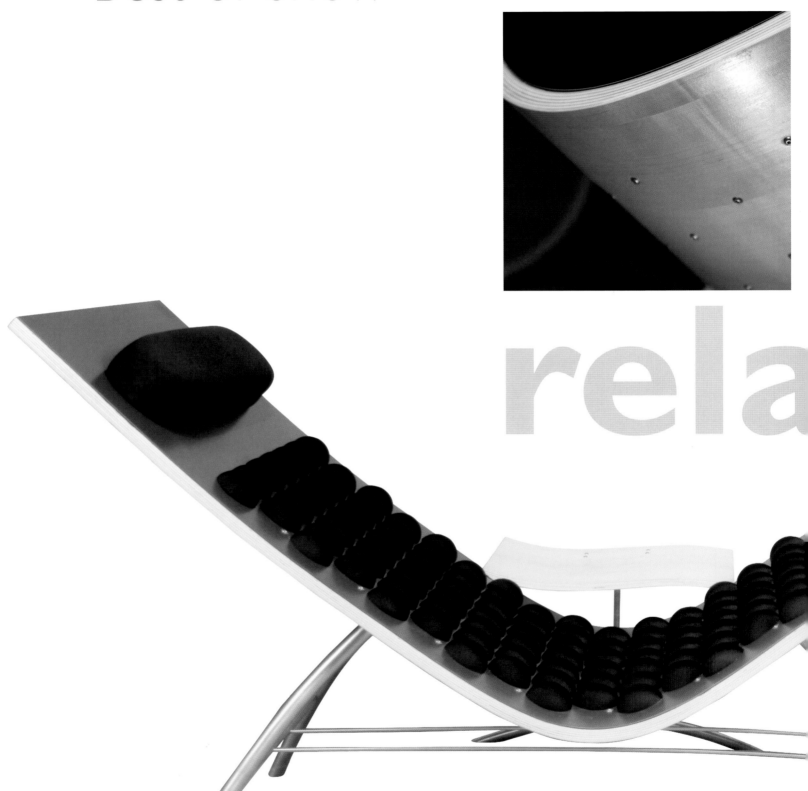

rela

Remington Ryan Wither • Savannah College of Art and Design

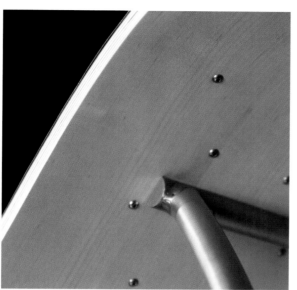

xation

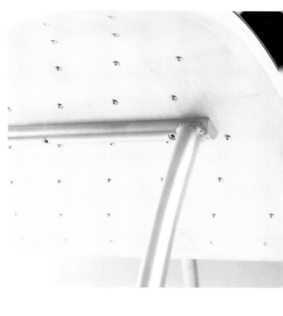

9

More information on page 72

The People's Choice

Ashley Nichole Hilton

The People's Choice Award is given for the furniture project that receives the most votes from those attending the AWFS®Fair. While many projects stood out for those reviewing the student design contest display area, Dinner Table, by Ashley Nichole Hilton was a clear favorite.

As Fair-goers realized Dinner Table was made by a student in high school, astonishment and appreciation for both her workmanship and design were often heard.

Ashley Nichole Hilton was a senior honors student at Cedar Ridge High School in Hillsborough, North Carolina when she produced Dinner Table and another entry, Chaise Lounge. Upon graduation, she successfully completed the WoodLINKS USA certificate and was awarded a scholarship from AWFS® for WoodLINKS USA graduates.

Ashley is attending Appalachian State University beginning Fall 2003 and pursuing a degree in Furniture Studies and Business. Upon graduation, Ashley plans on interning in the industry and hopes to eventually open her own custom furniture business.

People's Choice Award

Ashley Nichole Hilton • Cedar Ridge High School

Dinner Table

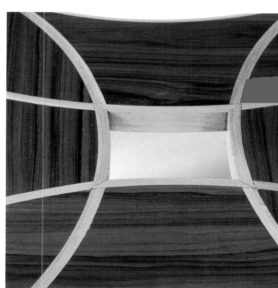

13

More information on page 35

Postsecondary

Creative

As colleges and universities are more likely to have design courses than the high schools, the Creative style at the Postsecondary level is very popular. It is the largest style group for 2003 with 23 finalists. An imaginative and clever cluster of pieces in the Casework/Cabinets category push the boundaries of what might at first come to mind for a category of this title. Two beautiful beds — one designed to dismantle for the relocating "nomadic professional," and another, the inspiration of an international adventure are found here, as is a light and airy woven wood screen that is illuminated and can be used open or closed. A contemporary vision of a grandfather clock is elegant, sleek, almost minimalist, yet unmistakably grandfather. The chair category is wildly diverse, ranging from personal variations on a traditional theme, such as the "Lewis Chair" to chairs that roll up into tables ("The Tambour Chair") to a seating for two that expands or contracts according to one's desire for (or lack of) closeness ("PROTEAN"). The Special Theme award was captured by an unusual adjustable book stand precisely engineered to balance large reading materials. With manufacturability in mind, most of the table entries were savvy to reproduction parameters, yet the designs and materials used were all encompassing. A finalist in the Upholstery category, Remington Wither took the Best of Show Award with "Relaxation," a unique sculptural lounging chair outfitted with halved massage balls supporting the lounger's body head to toe.

Traditional

There were seven finalists in the Postsecondary Traditional style group, and while the pieces reflect solid traditional forms and follow the contest criteria, there remains room for innovation within the traditional style. Gabriel Hugo Hernández' "Chippendale Lowboy Dresser" is classically styled and meticulously executed, while Casey Gloster's "Tracy's Music Nucleus" retains whimsical elements specific to the purpose of his piece — an elegant storage cabinet for music materials. Three rocking chairs made the finalist group, two drawing inspiration from Sam Maloof's classic rocker and one from the Arts and Crafts lineage. The traditional table entry, "Flip-Top Table," with its reversible pivoting top reveals a chessboard. Unlike more classic gaming tables, this one was created with an eye for easy manufacturability.

Casework/Cabinets

Chairs

Tables

Upholstery

Special Theme – Office Furniture of the Future

Postsecondary

Casework/Cabinets

Creative

Jon Plummer, Brigham Young University ....Japanese Convertible Bed

Kyle D. MacMillan, Pittsburg State University ...."La Grand" Humidor

Diane Creighton, Georgia Institute of Technology............Wood Maiden

Matthew A. Wiedmar, Jefferson Technical College ....SLOMAD

Drew Soderborg, Brigham Young University ....Grand Dad clock

Traditional

Gabriel Hugo Hernández,
Palomar College ....Chippendale Lowboy Dresser

Casey Gloster, Rockingham Community College ...Tracy's Music Nucleus

Matthew Gardner, Brigham Young University ....Arch Nightstand

First Place • Creative • Casework/Cabinets

Jon Plummer • Brigham Young University

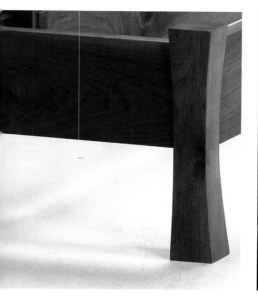

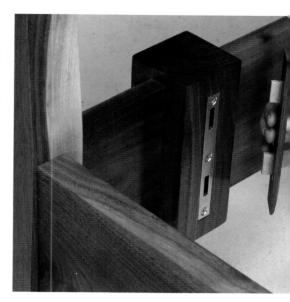

Japanese Convertible Bed

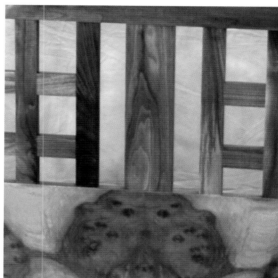

"I lived in Japan and found I was always interested in furniture, woodworking and Japanese design. The bed was designed after the Japanese *torri* gate found at the entrance to Buddhist shrines. The latticework in the headboard is reminiscent of the *shoji* doors commonly seen in Japan. Instead of repeating same-size squares within the lattice however, as is done with most Japanese *shoji*, I created a rectangular design while varying the sizes to create lines leading the focus to the center of the headboard.

Constructed of black walnut, bookmatched walnut burl veneer and sapwood, there is a beautiful natural contrast creating unique and interesting designs. The bed is convertible to either a king or queen size bed. The headboard has slots for both king and queen, while the footboard is collapsible to accommodate either sized box spring and mattress. As a king bed, the footboard has four legs and three rails. When converted to a queen, one of the legs and the center rail is removed.

Working with large pieces of wood was a challenge. Especially in the assembly, the large pieces required several hands, time and patience. I was most pleased with the overall appearance and feel of it. The Japanese feel and smooth curves are very appealing to me."

— Jon Plummer

19

Kyle D. MacMillan • Pittsburg State University

"La Grand" Humidor

" 'La Grand' Humidor was inspired by the appreciation of both pipes and cigars. Made of solid and veneered teak, 'La Grand' Humidor is comprised of several distinct features that resonate within its design.

The large solid teak legs, rather than being round, are made in the shape of tobacco leaves. These elevate the meticulously book-matched carcase (all panels have matching grain) off the ground. At night, lights glow underneath the top of the humidor to accentuate the shelving on both sides. These side shelves serve to accommodate pipes or personal belongings such as wallet, rings, watches, etc.

On the front, two beautifully curved doors swing open to reveal four solid Spanish cedar drawers that slide on precision dovetail drawer glides. Each drawer allows moisture to circulate around and within them through the special grooved pattern on the drawer bottoms, which is extremely important for maintaining cigar freshness. On top of the humidor and underneath the four drawers lie two inconspicuous compartments that are not moisture controlled. Instead, these are intended to house lighters, butane and other similar items.

Fabricated using mainly CNC machinery and shaper, 'La Grand' was designed to push the boundaries of what a humidor can be."

— Kyle D. MacMillan

Finalist • Creative • Casework/Cabinets

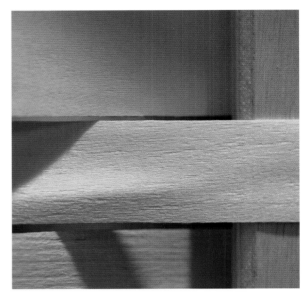

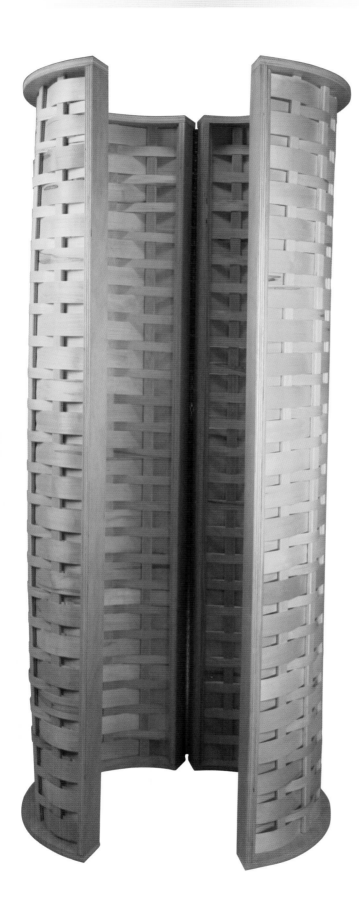

22

Diane Creighton • Georgia Institute of Technology

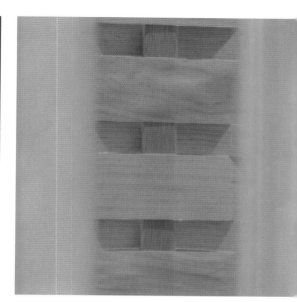

Wood Maiden

"The Wood Maiden reinvents the traditional three-panel screen. Woven wood 'fabric' allows light to shine through, so the Wood Maiden separates and connects space both physically and visually. It can be used or viewed in both open and closed positions.

Standing seven feet tall, the birch plywood frame holds a delicately woven fabric of maple veneer, which gently dissipates light in lovely patterns. When fully opened, the screen spans four feet, physically separating space while visually allowing light to penetrate and connect space. When fully closed, the wooden column creates a full circle around which to walk and view. A six-foot piano hinge allows for easy operation while bottom-mounted gliders ensure smooth movement."

– Diane Creighton

Matthew A. Wiedmar • Jefferson Technical College

SLOMAD

"The inspiration for this bed design came from a personal challenge to produce a bed for the young professional, one with style and class. It would have manufacturability for middle to high-end markets, and appeal to both traditional as well as contemporary furniture lovers. The underlying appeal of the concept I call "SLOMAD" is that, unlike traditional sleigh beds, it can be shipped ready to assemble (RTA) and also be assembled by one person. The name "SLOMAD" evolved from the very concept of a piece of furniture made for the nomadic professional.

In taking this particular piece from concept to manufacture, several problems needed to be resolved: bending the wood, maintaining the structural integrity of the piece and the disassembly construction. I decided to focus on the head and footboard assemblies. To ensure that the slats wouldn't move when installing the stabilizing rod and spacers, I used dowel rails. This element allows for the one-person assembly and lends a great deal of structural integrity. The slats were produced using a 7-ply poplar core laminated with lyptus veneer.

The bed frame was produced with a plantation hardwood called lyptus. This species was chosen for its rich look, exceptional finishing characteristics, and more than competitive price tag."

— Matthew A. Wiedmar

Finalist • Creative • Casework/Cabinets

Drew Soderborg • Brigham Young University

Grand Dad Clock

"When I began to design this grandfather clock, I wanted to create a clock with a more contemporary feel. The form of the clock has been simplified almost to the bare bones. Most of the decoration found on more traditional grandfather clocks is gone.

It is the motion in a grandfather clock that is intriguing to me. The rotating of the hands and the swinging of the pendulum are what makes a grandfather clock different from all other furniture. For this reason, I decided to focus on these parts and to let them be more exposed.

The box and shelves are made of cherry, while the legs are made of maple. The slight curve on the legs was rough-cut on the bandsaw and then finished with an adjustable sole hand plane. The bottom of the clock is open to give a clear view of the pendulum. The pendulum, face and hands are of brushed aluminum. The more contemporary dots and dashes are used on the face instead of numbers, to complement the modern look of the clock. The face itself is made of natural slate."

– Drew Soderborg

Gabriel Hugo Hernández • Palomar College

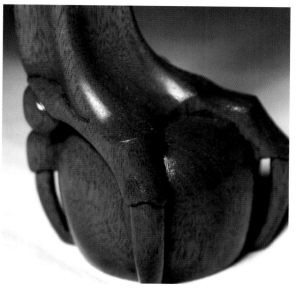

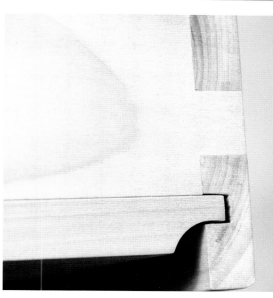

Chippendale Lowboy Dresser

"I was inspired when I saw an authentic Chippendale at an antique store. I've been working in wood for six years but have been exposed to woodworking since childhood. I drew sketches of the piece, making a few changes from the one I saw in the store. I made all four legs with the ball and claw style. I designed the carving for the front drawer, with matching carvings on the front, sides and back of the dressing table. Designing the piece was the most challenging aspect of creating the Chippendale.

The Chippendale is made from Honduras mahogany on the frame, legs and the top. I used poplar inside of the drawers, creating a nice contrast on the dovetail joints. The top was not glued down and can easily be detached by unscrewing the bolts. I used mortise and tenon to join the panels to the legs. The details on the drawer front, the sides and the back, as well as the ball and claw feet, were all handcarved. I finished the Chippendale with oil and added brass pulls.

I am most proud of the legs, especially the details in the clawed feet. The Chippendale is now displayed in the entrance hallway of my home."

— Gabriel Hugo Hernández

Casey Gloster · Rockingham Community College

Tracy's Music Nucleus

"This furniture piece is motivated by the needs of a musician. She required filing storage for large quantities of sheet music and other materials related to playing and teaching the harp.

This piece incorporates a two-part construction. The top is a bookcase with arched door fronts framed by fluted columns, constructed of butternut and accented with American walnut. The base is a chest of drawers with an adaptation making each drawer a double file storage system. This also has fluted sides ending in cabriole-style legs. It is made of butternut and walnut accents with a walnut top. Custom designed, handcarved solid brass pulls in a musical motif are used; the musical motif is found throughout both parts. Both pieces are built with mortise and tenon joinery filled with frame and panel sections. The frame and panels work well for ease of assembly in gluing and add more detail to the piece than flat sides. This construction allows for wood movement without distracting from aesthetics.

The design is bold and sensuous with grand arches and full volutes accented with rich, strong, contrasting colors. I hope this project evokes the emotions given to the furniture of the eighteenth century."

– Casey Gloster

Matthew Gardner • Brigham Young University

Arch
Nightstand

"The Arch Nightstand plays off themes in my Arch Bed Frame, which include visual references to Shaker simplicity and arches of the classical era. The nightstand features straight lines with a horizontal emphasis, a feeling of airiness and strong symmetry. I have used a contrast of bird's-eye maple and cherry woods, in a frame and panel construction. The posts are resawn and book matched, as are the side and back panels.

The doors, drawers and front stretcher curve outward from the legs. The top of the arch in the drawer front doubles as the drawer pull. French dovetails were cut prior to the curved grooves created with a dado blade on the tablesaw.

Shaping the cupboard doors was complicated. The doors were designed to sit within the frame set by the legs, stretcher and drawer frame. The tops of the doors meet the curved bottom of the drawer front. The drawer front and the doors, when closed, are designed to cover the drawer ring. These three facts combined to make my head do some footwork before cutting the wood.

One of my favorite aspects of the design is the hidden compartment inside the cupboard. Just lift the lid — what appears to be the bottom of the cupboard — to find cookies stashed for a midnight snack.

– Matthew Gardner

33

Postsecondary

Chairs

Creative

Brian M. Sanderson, Brigham Young University ....The Tambour Chair

Jeffrey Foye, Cerritos College ....Box Joint Bench

Jane Lee, Rhode Island School of Design ....Red

Michael Craigdallie, Selkirk College ....The Lewis Chair

Min J. Lee, Art Center College of Design ....Bayou

Justin Porcano, Art Center College of Design.....................PROTEAN

Traditional

Eugene T. Morgan, Fullerton College ....The Morgan Rocker

David Mootchnik, Cerritos College ....Mahogany Rocking Chair

James L. Ryckebosch, Fullerton College ....Rocking Chair

First Place • Creative • Chairs

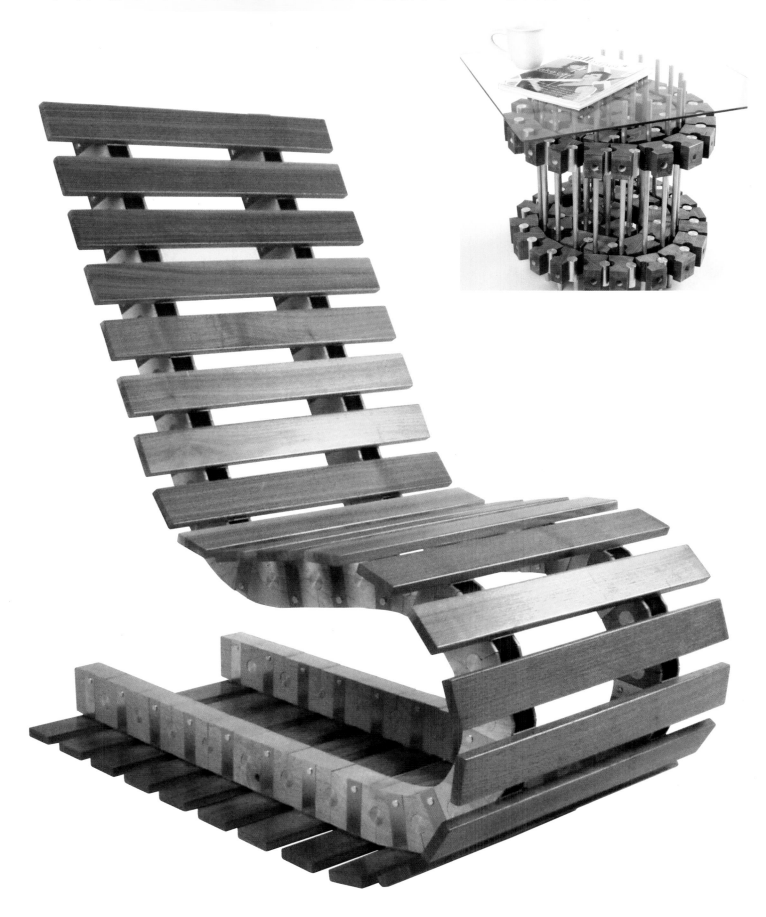

Brian M. Sanderson • Brigham Young University

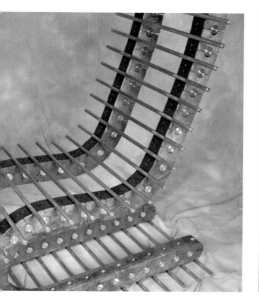

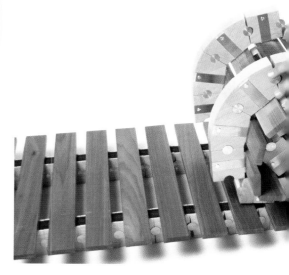

The Tambour Chair

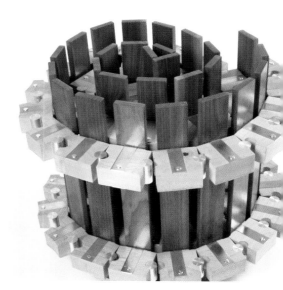

"While contemplating the concept of bridging the technology gap between older and younger generations, I had the idea of bridging two existing furniture designs. The roll-top desk has always brought thoughts of tradition, simplicity, sturdiness, and longevity, thoughts that I associate with my grandparents. Gerrit Rietveld's Zig Zag Chair was designed in 1934, yet it has impressed me as being very modern. With its simplicity, diagonal lines, visual tension, and creative construction, it refuses to be confined by tradition, much like today's younger generations.

I decided on a chair that would implement the wood and the tambour of the roll-top desk, as well as the modern design of the Zig-Zag Chair. After two mock-ups and a working prototype, I had the Tambour Chair.

The most unique aspect of the chair is that it rolls up — for storage, for show, or for use as an end table underneath a flat piece of glass. The construction consists of a solid white maple frame, walnut slats, aluminum keys and hardware, and high-strength strapping. Although initially time consuming, the design is fairly simple and could be manufactured quite efficiently.

The Tambour Chair can be made from lightweight composites weighing one tenth as much, with a rolled size one third the diameter."

Domestic and international patents pending.

— Brian M. Sanderson

Honorable Mention • Creative • Chairs

Jeffrey Foye • Cerritos College

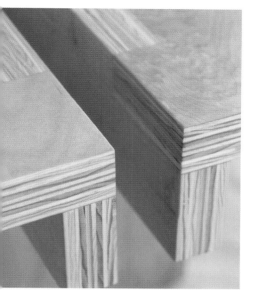
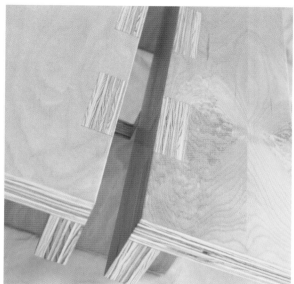
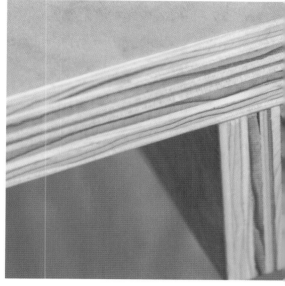

Box Joint Bench

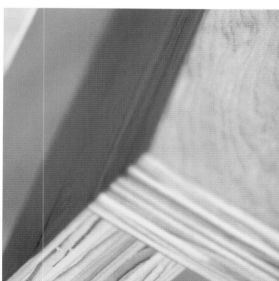

"My work arises from mid-twentieth century modernism, in the economy of materials and in allowing the material and construction to come forward as decoration. I approached this project with a focus on the nature of the material together with the basic function of a bench.

Made of double laminated five-core birch plywood, this bench is two flanges running parallel to form the top, with two parallel vertical elements to form the legs. The top of the flanges form the seat while the vertical element provides triangulation strength. Meeting along the center of the bench, the flanges leave a space where most designs classically concentrate strength. The box joint features the laminated core of the material in a nice rhythmic pattern along the joint. The bench adds to that rhythm by mirroring the joints of the two halves, featuring the core element generally hidden in cabinets or case goods.

My original intention was to challenge myself with new techniques. I arrived at creating a pattern to follow with a flush-trim bit on a router to make the precise and large box joint. I now had an easily mass producible design. Inexpensive material combined with manufacturability created a piece that is equally functional as seating, as a table, or simply as art."

– Jeffrey Foye

Michael Craigdallie • Selkirk College

The Lewis Chair

"This chair is part of a dining set of table and six chairs as a 'commission' from a good friend of mine, and hence bears his name. The process started with ideas and sketches. From those, a scale model was built to help determine size and proportions. Some forty or so jigs, carriers and templates were required to build this chair and were made as the prototype was built.

This chair, built entirely of black walnut, was designed to have a light visual appearance without compromising the structural integrity of the piece. Therefore all of the structural joinery in the frame is traditional mortise and tenon. The side rails are set in from the side of the chair. This was done for two reasons: it allowed me to connect the rails to the front and back cross rails at ninety degrees which simplified the joinery by eliminating angles. This also gave the seat the appearance that it was floating. To add to the look that it is floating, the seat is cut around the legs and is only connected to the side rails. The seat was carved with a curve for comfort. The curve in the back rails offer lumbar support."

— Michael Craigdallie

Finalist • Creative • Chairs

Jane Lee • Rhode Island School of Design

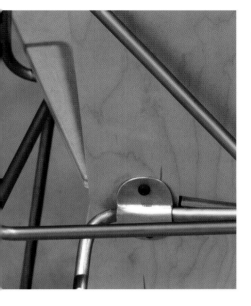

Red

"Red is an easy chair that uses an innovative joining system and structure to make the piece aesthetically appealing, as well as to allow for flexible movement. Lines and colors inspire me – the overall design of Red accentuates the linear quality of the red fabric and also reflects the structural elements.

The materials used are 1/8" birch plywood, red denim fabric, and 3/8" steel rods. Three sheets of 1/8" birch plywood are laminated together with a sheet of red fabric in between the layers of the wood. The continuous red line around the edges of the chair is created by this technique. The chair is divided into the left panels and the right panels with a gap that shows the fabric running down the middle. The triangular bends of the steel rods in the back of the chair – the 'elbows' – are purposely shaped in such fashion. When one sits in the chair, these elbows torque and push the left and right wooden panels inward to make the chair fit more comfortably around one's back. The steel rods were bent and welded together at several places."

– Jane Lee

Finalist • Creative • Chairs

Min J. Lee • Art Center College of Design

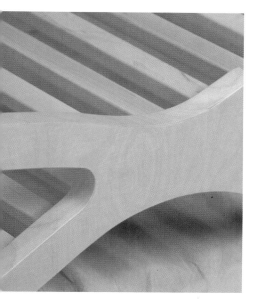

Bayou

"Bayou is a chaise lounge that embodies a combination of the Asian ground-sitting and western seating lifestyles. Its body touches the ground and gives you a totally different sitting experience. It also can be positioned backwards so you put your legs up, which is good for your tired and swollen legs.

The two side panels are made out of natural 18-ply maple plywood. The woodgrain is emphasized by the light touch of wood finish. The flowing shape of the side panels are connected with hard maple crossbars. An industrial felt piece was used for the pad.

The sinuous and continuous bodylines of Bayou are developed after the shape of water. The concept of this chaise lounge was to bring the contour of nature into the home. Bayou, which means a body of water such as a creek or small river, is lightweight for easy lifting and can be stored vertically against the wall. After taking off the felt piece, it can be left outside as outdoor furniture. Its flexibility in materials, colors, and textures suits many people's needs."

— Min J. Lee

Finalist • Creative • Chairs

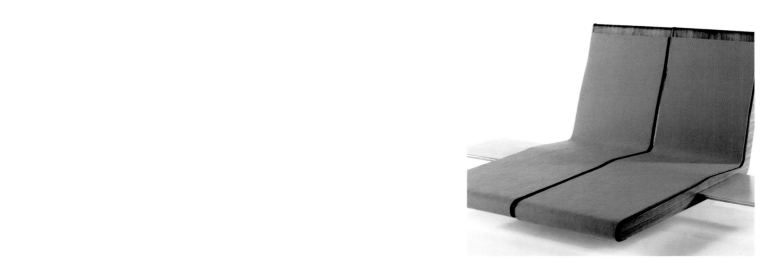

Justin Porcano • Art Center College of Design

PROTEAN

"The name of my furniture piece is PROTEAN. Loosely defined, protean is the ability to change form and meaning. PROTEAN is basically two chairs that slide on a birch plank, which also serves as end, middle or side tables. PROTEAN is held slightly above the ground on aluminum legs with rolling pin-like castors.

The concept came from the exploration of the social tensions that can exist when sitting on a love seat. The dimensions of a love seat can be a little too personal at times, ignoring the need for our own personal space. The PROTEAN chair allows you to adjust the seating, depending on the situation you desire, by simply sliding them closer together or apart.

The bulk of the chair was constructed by CNC routing 1/4" Baltic plywood slats, which fit together into a 3" by 3" grid. Once assembled, the pieces were hand planed to get a clean even surface. The chairs were then wrapped in bending poplar, sanded and veneered with walnut. The 5/8" industrial felt was mounted in the appropriate locations to add comfort to the chair."

— Justin Porcano

First Place • Traditional • Chairs

Eugene T. Morgan • Fullerton College

The Morgan Rocker

"The birth of my first grandchild, Morgan Elizabeth, inspired the desire for the perfect rocking chair. I've been woodworking for over twenty years and felt up to the challenge. My visit to Sam Maloof's workshop inspired the design for my much needed rocking chair.

The use of Maloof's visible joints technique was something I knew I wanted to incorporate into my design. Along with many other adopted features, I incorporated Maloof's style of front leg joints and the laminated rockers. I designed the rear leg-to-seat joints. This involved use of two large dovetail tenons. The concept of the arms coming off the rear leg frames and the sides allowed a butted joint. The final original concept was to put a roman nose on the front of the seat. The most difficult challenges were the arms and the diamond accents, which I felt were necessary to the design. The overall use of diamond maple plugs was a final touch that gave an overall elegance to the rocking chair."

— Eugene T. Morgan

David Mootchnik • Cerritos College

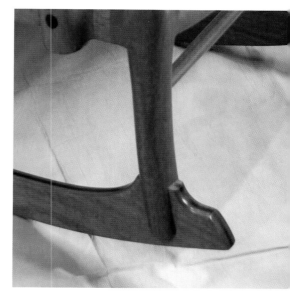
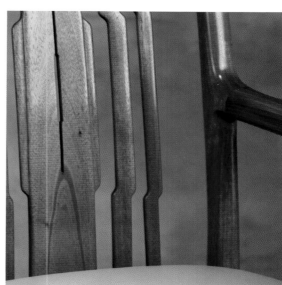

Mahogany Rocking Chair

"This is a contemporary rocking chair with an arts and craft flavor. It's primarily made of Honduras mahogany with accents of Peruvian walnut and black walnut. I chose to use an upholstered seat covered in leather as a final touch.

The construction techniques used were mortise, tenon and doweled joints. Arm supports were attached with a cogged dado and brass bolts (the bolts are hidden). A stretcher braces the front legs and the rockers are laminated for strength and design. The back consists of one wide splat and four slats with the splat curved in two directions for comfort. These are all mortised into the back and crest rail. The crest rail was fitted and held with wood screws and covered with ebony plugs. Finally, it was finished to a glossy surface with an oil varnish.

As a final piece, I am happy with the overall construction. It's very well balanced and comfortable."

– David Mootchnik

Finalist • Traditional • Chairs

James L. Ryckebosch • Fullerton College

Rocking Chair

"As a project challenge I decided to create a rocking chair based on Sam Maloof's working methods and designs. I've been working in wood for over eight years and I just wanted to see if I could do it.

I used walnut with accents of ebony in the rocker. Parts were reinforced with stainless steel screws and covered with ebony plugs. I made a few modifications from Sam Maloof's methods. I chose to make the legs rectangular with rounded edges and tapered at the bottom. The front leg-seat joints were also modified. I used a 1" diameter bit to make the joints, creating a slightly larger joint. This allowed me to use fewer screws to reinforce the joint. The rear leg-seat joints were the most difficult challenge for me.

The chair has a lot of fine details that are subtle. I would say after the rocking chair was completed I was happiest with the seat joints and was very appreciative of the challenges I was able to overcome."

– James L. Ryckebosch

Postsecondary

Tables

Creative

Traditional

First Place • Creative • Tables

Brittany Davis • Brigham Young University

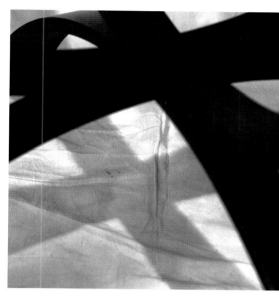

Zhe Table

"This project is based on a stylization of the Russian letter Ж, pronounced 'Zhe.' A feature that makes this table interesting is its deceptive delicacy, but surprising strength.

It is constructed of four arcs of the same radius, connected in the center by a dadoed joint and four hidden screws and fasteners. Each arc is made of six layers of white oak laminated together. The oak was first steamed and allowed to dry in a two-part form, then glued with polyurethane glue, and again clamped into the form and allowed to dry overnight. The pieces were then cut to taper toward the center and flare slightly at the ends. The dado joint was cut using a router with a special jig and the hidden fasteners were inserted.

The arcs were stained, first using a water-based stain, followed by an oil stain, then lacquered, glazed with an oil-based glaze and finally lacquered again.

I chose a glass top for the table so that the joint would be visible. This piece is completely collapsible and easily reassembled using only an allen wrench."

— Brittany Davis

Honorable Mention • Creative • Tables

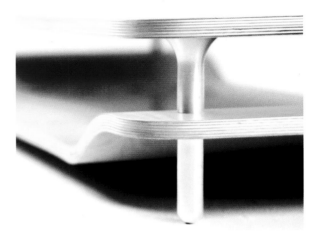

Katie Richardson • Brigham Young University

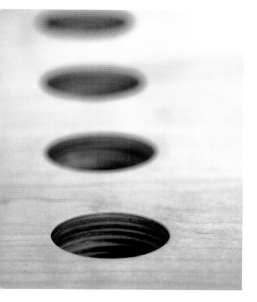
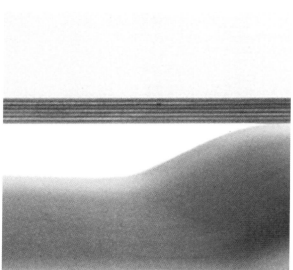

Fiora

"When I designed Fiora I tried to emulate the warm feelings of springtime. I have always loved the feeling of walking barefoot through the green grass and feeling the sun warm my face. The Fiora engages this emotion when you place her in your home. Fiora is designed to support a small flower vase to continue the theme of springtime, and the hand-blown vase adds a quality of freshness.

The Fiora was designed for manufacturability with minimal waste and maximum use of materials. A standard 5' by 5' by 3/4" sheet of Baltic birch plywood will create three tops. The bent shelf is composed of two 5' by 5' by 1/8" piece of Baltic birch plywood cut into thirds, each with only enough excess to clean up the edges. For a final added elegance, each shelf is covered with a maple veneer.

Fiora knocks down with great ease, which allows for easy shipment. Once the buyer takes Fiora home, she is quickly put together. The turned aluminum legs attach to the underside of the table with a rare earth magnet. The second shelf is suspended between the threaded portion of the legs. When all legs are securely tightened you have a new coffee table that is both elegant and easily put together."

– Katie Richardson

Finalist • Creative • Tables

Benjamin John Purrenhage • Western Michigan University

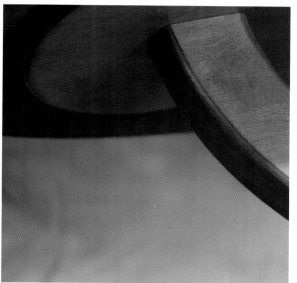
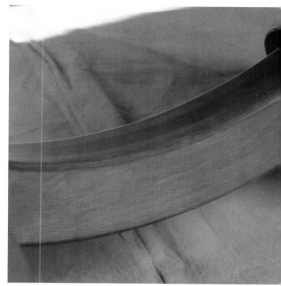

Elise

"The Elise table was designed as a beautifully functional table. It can be easily taken apart for transportation or cleaning. Every element of the Elise table has an elliptical form. The lines created by the tabletop are mirrored throughout the base.

The heavy top is made from 3/4" black absolute granite and the base is constructed from solid cherry sandwiched between two pieces of Baltic plywood. By using plywood in combination with solid wood, the arcs of the base meet each other at lap joints with a 45 degree chamfer that aids in strength and stability. The top is attached to the base with locking hardware and can be easily removed. A dark stain was applied to the wood to coordinate with the dark granite top. Polyurethane lacquer was then applied to protect the wood from moisture. The manufacturing cost was kept low compared to other bent wood tables.

The Elise table is elegant as well as functional. It gives the coffee table a new and exciting look while still remaining in the budget of most consumers."

— Benjamin John Purrenhage

Finalist • Creative • Tables

Andrew Housley • Brigham Young University

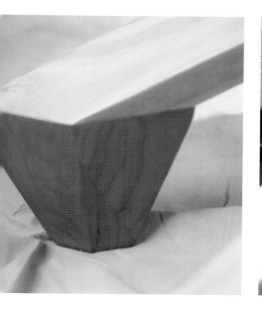

Arch
Coffee Table

"Since childhood arches have fascinated me. I was intrigued by how large arched bridges could span seemingly immense divides. I remember as a child seeing Glen Canyon Dam and the bridge in front of the dam exploiting the strength of wide flat arches. That form eventually moved me to create the supporting structure for this table. Another inspiration was a public television program showing how traditional small boat builders used steamed wood bending. Wood is such a beautiful material. The idea that it could not only be cut and sculpted, but also bent, instilled within me the desire to explore the possibilities.

In the table's design, I mimicked the form of the arched, solid ash in the inlays on the cherry tabletop. I made a template for the handheld plunge-router to be pulled along as the inlay grooves were cut. I tilted the legs in towards the center to conceal the matting between the top and the legs. From many angles, this concealment creates the impression that the top is balancing precariously on an unseen fulcrum, creating curiosity. It invites you to come closer to investigate, bringing the arches closer for inspection. In order to terminate and contrast the flowing lines of the arches, the legs come to sudden points where they meet the sharp, angular cherry feet."

– Andrew Housley

Finalist • Creative • Tables

Jason W. Tippetts • Brigham Young University

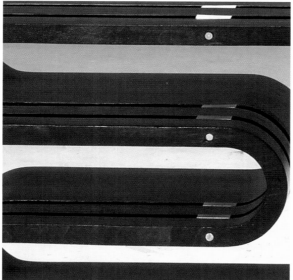
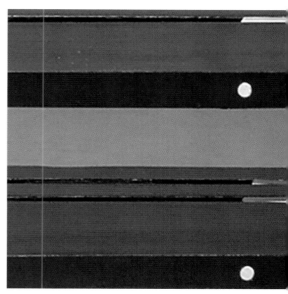

Ribbon Coffee

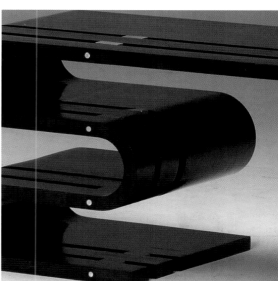

"Ribbon Coffee was designed to function as a contemporary and conceptual design. Primarily, it is a studio piece, an experiment in craftsmanship and form.

Ribbon Coffee was originally intended to be a bent piece of black acrylic. As my idea moved from a sketch to the worktable, that aspect changed. The silky ribbon-like form, with its tight curves on the support legs, would not provide the support the table would need. Instead, the same profile was cut out several times and laminated together to create the desired form.

The silhouettes were CNC routed out of 5' by 5' pieces of 3/4" birch plywood. Using an onionskin process, the shapes were perforated into the wood, then, using a hand router, they were punched out. The rest was hours of sanding and finishing. A black dye mixed with a red mahogany gel-stain provided the deep richness in color. I used a high gloss polyurethane finish to protect it.

What about the wasted material? A similar concept will employ the negative space material, left over after punching out the silhouettes, in another table design. Close to 80 percent of the material will have been used, allowing me to split the cost of the material and the CNC work between two pieces of furniture."

— Jason W. Tippetts

Finalist • Creative • Tables

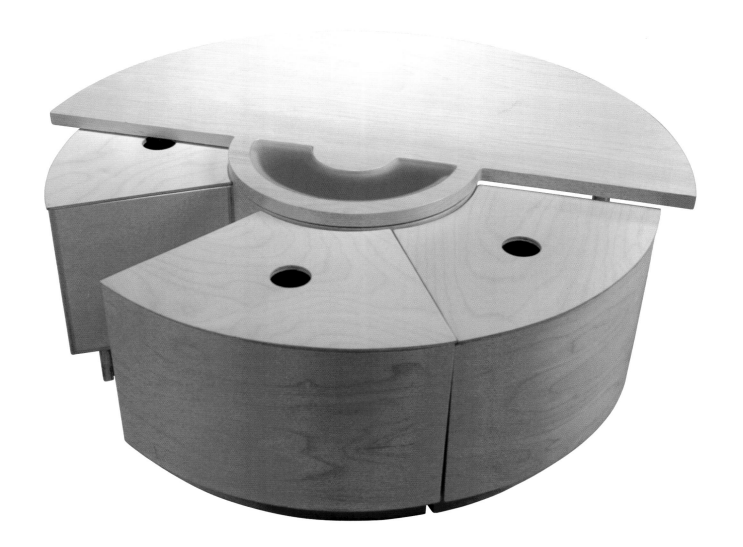

Min J. Lee • Art Center College of Design

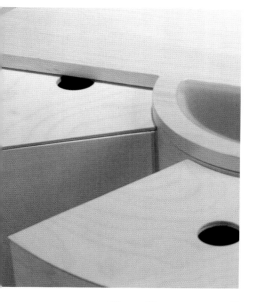
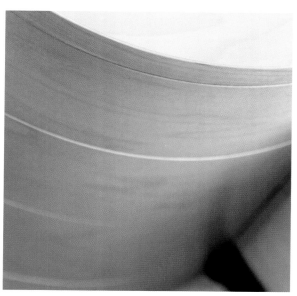
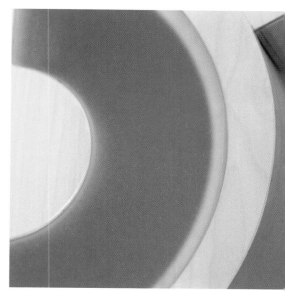

Motion T Table

"The Motion T Table is a multi-functional table that embodies a metaphor of togetherness and the Asian ground-sitting lifestyle. Therefore, it is only 12" tall.

Over 90 percent of this table is made of natural maple plywood. The woodgrain is emphasized by a light touch of wood finish. Motion T consists of a revolving top and a center cylinder storage. The center cylinder is made of two layers of 6-ply maple musical drum shells. Three cylinder storage compartments are each attached to different rings of the outside cylinder compartment to allow for individual rotations. To keep the table lightweight, 1/2" plywood is used for the skeleton of the top, and then laminated with 1/8" plywood. The revolving top is supported by two 3/4" aluminum legs with wheels, and can be expanded to a full circle.

With this semi-circular revolving table, you can lean, read, work, eat, study, play and simply live on and around it, by yourself or with another person. From young children to college students living in cramped spaces, the Motion T Table is a lovely feature that allows one to be organized, yet exercise an inner playfulness."

– Min J. Lee

68

John Donley • Brigham Young University

Flip-Top Table

"This table has a very traditional style with clean solid joinery for those who enjoy quality furniture. In order to keep a more traditional style, I made the table out of walnut, which adds to the design and matches the chessboard side, as well as white maple.

I designed the tabletop frame so that there is no set way it has to face. This design makes it easier to mass-produce. The one side of the tabletop center is a book match veneer with character and figuration, while the other side is a chessboard. The tabletop center pivots on two pins in the center of it and is held in place by four custom maple pins that are attached to the front and back aprons. The pins are 1" square by 2 1/2" long. Custom walnut brackets hold the pins up flush with the bottom of the tabletop.

This table would be fairly easy to mass-produce because it does not have very many different pieces to construct. The table is 2' by 2' and 30" tall."

– John Donley

Postsecondary

Upholstery

Creative

First Place • Creative • Upholstery

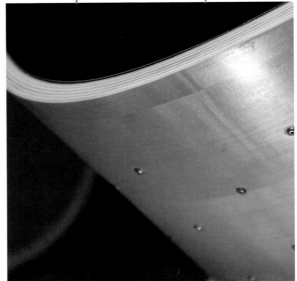

Remington Ryan Wither • Savannah College of Art and Design

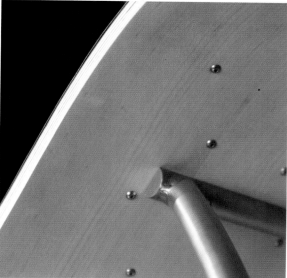

Relaxation

"Relaxation was inspired by the hypnotic feeling I get when watching waves on the Pacific Ocean. The idea of balls penetrating steel was an evolving experiment, realized in the wee hours of the morning. Relaxation holds you in a contemplative and secure position while you regroup and reflect on what really matters in life; the upholstered hemispheres contribute to a soothing sensation as pressure points along your body are activated.

The structure was made by vacuum forming and bending poplar plywood; the form was the result of two weeks of user testing on a mocked-up MDF lounge chair. Over a dozen different balls were used in prototyping the chair to achieve the desired feeling. The wooden carcass was skinned with mild steel that was water-jet cut to fit over eight dozen massage balls cut into halves. Two layers of spandex are sandwiched between the steel and wood by over 150 sex bolts. The fabric had to be cauterized at each individual bolt. The headrest is upholstered foam with magnets recessed into a plywood structure. The entire form is supported on legs of aluminum tubing, carefully machined and welded to fit the exact angles of the curve. The aluminum and mild steel are powder coated to ensure a scratch resistant surface."

— Remington Ryan Wither

Susan Yoo • Art Center College of Design

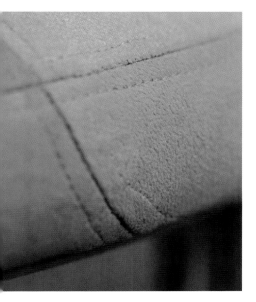
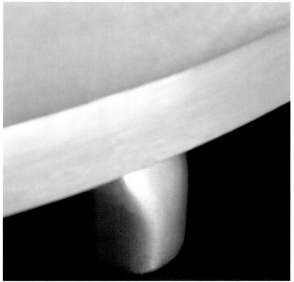
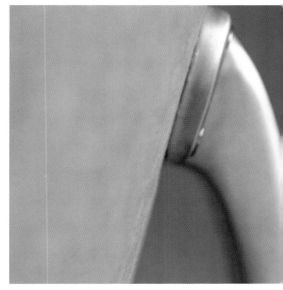

Lazy Susan Chair

"The Lazy Susan Chair was designed to provide comfort to all kinds of people... tall, short, big and small. It features a large 36" seating area to provide more sitting options and comfort. A round sitting element consists of a backrest and an armrest proportioned for support and comfort.

The chair's main structure, the frame, was constructed of wood. The frame of the seating part was CNC-cut of 1" Baltic plywood sheets. The construction of the frame took the shape of a barrel, which allowed me to minimize the weight of the piece. A lazy susan track was added to the bottom of the frame; this was attached to an additional circular panel on which the legs were attached. The lazy susan track supports the chair and enables a smooth 360-degree rotation.

The back and armrest required a 150-degree curvature, fabricated by layering 1/8" bending plywood sheets. The glued layers provide thickness and strength.

The piece was upholstered in ultra suede due to its soft feel. The satin-finish aluminum castings and rim around the chair were a perfect accent to bring all the chair elements together."

— Susan Yoo

Finalist • Creative • Upholstery

Aira Loren Rogers • Auburn University

Hug Chair

"The Hug Chair was named for its comforting way of enveloping the user like a big hug. The overall design was inspired by the Gulf of Mexico where I grew up, mimicking the curvature and soft lines of seashells. I chose the color and texture of the fabric for the resemblance to the ocean. The nap on the cushions is alternated vertically so that light creates a wave effect across the slightly reflective fabric. The Hug Chair was entirely hand stitched by the designer. These elements create a perfect lounging and relaxation chair.

The chair has an anthropometrically correct 17" high seat pan. The seat depth and width are both 24", allowing room for users of all sizes. The slightly angled back encourages a relaxed yet alert posture. The sage blue-grey upholstery cloth is a durable plush cotton/polyester with a soft textured finish and a large corduroy-like wale to create a sophisticated yet inviting look.

The makore (African cherry) feet, with their rich warm hues, complement the fabric's cool neutral color, bringing out hidden red tones in the cloth. The ribbed interior skeleton is made from 3/4" luan plywood. In a production setting, the chair would be constructed using traditional techniques for an overstuffed chair."

— Aira Loren Rogers

Postsecondary

Special Theme

Creative

Armond Tavianini • Fullerton College

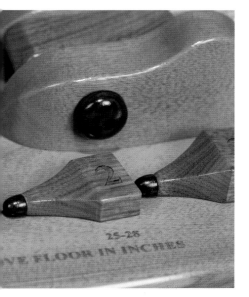

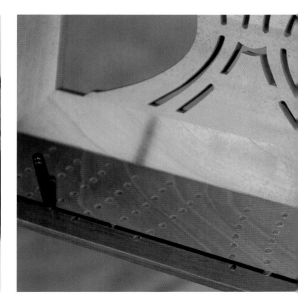

Three-Way Adjustable Book Stand

"I designed this piece to support large or cumbersome printed material while being read or referenced. The stand can be adjusted in a variety of sitting or reclining positions. The inspiration for this stand came as I was reading a 5 lb. book in a reclining chair, constantly shifting my arms and upper body in an effort to avoid fatigue.

The design of the main pivot connecting the two support arms was the most challenging and incorporated the use of two wood threaded, donut shaped ebony nuts and a macassar wood 3/4" threaded bolt. The second challenge was finding the correct length of the two support arms to ensure that the stand would remain stable and upright in the various configurations. This required a combination of mathematics and many trials. The third challenge was the design and sizing of the four height-adjusting blocks tucked into the mahogany base.

Even though the stand has a light and airy appearance, it is surprisingly stable. It could also function as a music stand for players of a host of instruments because of its unique design. However its overriding strength is in supporting material weighing considerably more than sheet music.

Materials used are as follows: Honduras mahogany, walnut, macassar ebony, exterior Baltic birch and brass rod."

— Armond Tavianini

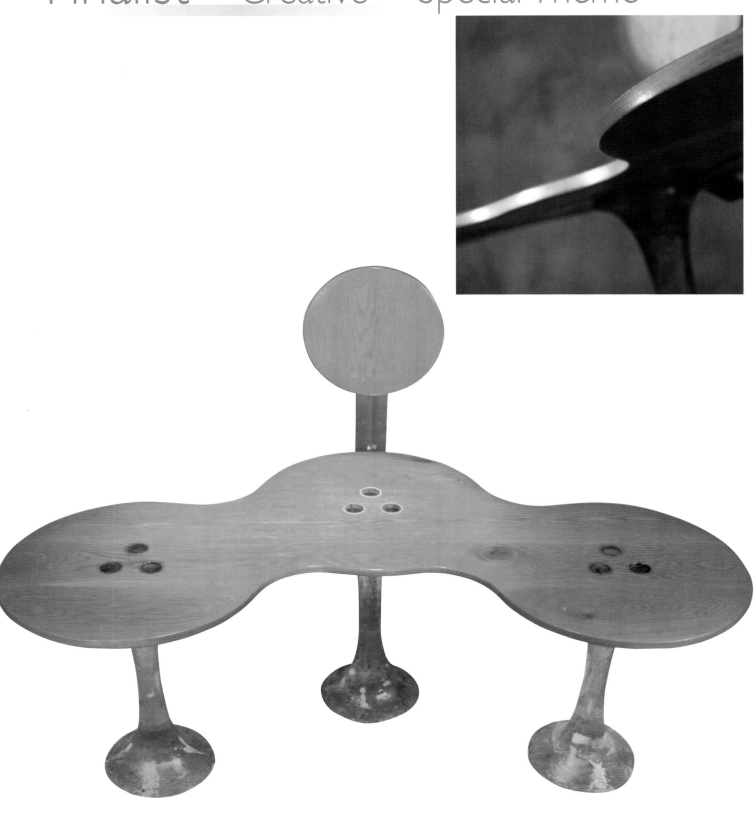

82

Ryan Sprouse Dart • Brigham Young University

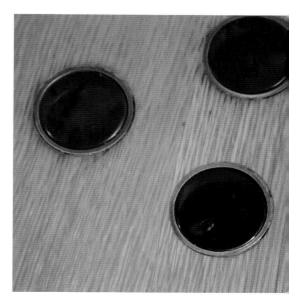

The Corner Bench

"Designed for metropolitan areas where space is tight, the Corner Bench uses the corner of a room, directing the seated people's attention to the center of the room or to each other. My inspiration was to simplify the piece, yet catch the eye. This piece was designed for younger people who don't have much space, but still like clean lines with a unique flair; for people who hop on their beach-cruisers or head to book stores or the local café to hear their friend play the guitar.

I used many special techniques. For example, the legs of the Corner Bench were made from plaster molds into which I poured the resin. I also left the legs with the pits and valleys — a rough finish designed to create more depth to the legs. LED lights dance on these surfaces fusing art with function. The wood pieces, all of white oak, were handshaped. I used a center back rest on the bench to give more dimension to the piece and to accent the corner of a room where it is designed to be placed. While those seated on the side have the wall to lean against, the person in the middle (corner) seat has the center back rest to lean against."

— Ryan Sprouse Dart

John VanErem • Pittsburg State University

Turning Point

"This desk suits the 'Office Furniture of the Future' theme because its design features are unlike any traditional office furniture style. Its utilization of space capitalizes on the needs and concerns of future offices. It isn't just a stand-alone desk; it also functions as a conference table. The top swivels 360 degrees on an off-center pivot, allowing it to sit in front of you or open fully for conference use.

The desk is made with an ultra-light MDF covered with Nevamar laminates, and smoked tempered glass doors. The drawers swing independently on a unique pivot rod that houses anti-friction material called 'trespa.' The drawers are equipped with Hafele's Dialock, a wireless locking system. Space is maximized between the drawers and the shelves with storage area.

Thanks to AutoCAD, this design became what it is today. I began with a very simple design and it grew to become something great. I had a lot of fun designing this in 3D and I have to say I learned a lot. It is hard to design office furniture of the future because the world changes so much everyday. Yet, I feel my design is not only functional today but will be functional well into the future."

– John VanErem

85

High School

Creative

Playful, prudent and enigmatic describe the twelve Creative pieces at the high school level. The degree of challenge that these pieces must have posed to each of the students is noteworthy. A cleverly constructed bed that houses compartments in the framework is a visual treat. "Celestial Bed," with its arcing sun, moon and stars emits the feeling of a Fourth of July fireworks. "Cerca del Soñador," a headboard, expands and shrinks to fit both king and queen beds (and saves on shipping costs). "Music Stand" by Wes Wegner is delicate and lovely – an etude in wood. The People's Choice is in this group – "Dinner Table" by Ashley Hilton. Matching the pie-shaped veneers on this round table is a feat that would be admirable of an experienced professional let alone a student. "Executive Desk" shows a refreshing and refined use of wood choices and inclusion of desk compartments and convenient features. "Floating Book/Display Case" is an imaginative design incorporating veneer, sheet stainless steel, birch ply and painted poplar. The high school projects left no stone unturned in terms of the scope and complexity of projects. The bar has been driven very high by this year's finalists and will constitute a significant challenge to applicants in 2005.

Traditional

Nine Traditional pieces at the high school level reveal a sound command of woodworking craft, both from a hand skills perspective as well as familiarity with and incorporation of the use of machine tools and CNC equipment. From sophisticated cabinets and vanities to storage chests, drop-leaf tables and upholstered chaises, an enormous exhibition of skill is evident in this high school group. The aptly named "Weightless Mammoth" is an extraordinary undertaking, a large, commanding hutch-style cabinet nonetheless supported by delicate looking and shapely legs. The attention to wood surfacing is immediate on "Oval Walnut Vanity," a subtle but rich use of walnut and walnut burl. Begging to be tested is "Chaise Lounge," a plushly upholstered chaise with a sculpted back.

Casework/Cabinets

Tables

Upholstery

Special Theme – Office Furniture of the Future

High School

Casework/Cabinets

Creative

Traditional

First Place • Creative • Casework/Cabinets

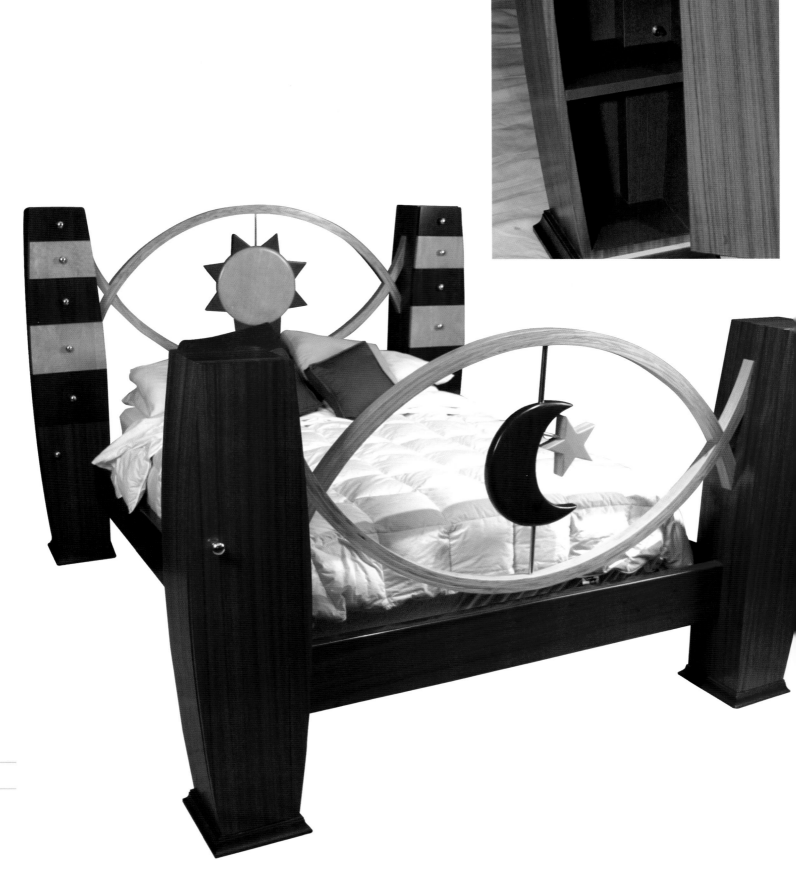

Katelyn Ander • Cedar Ridge High School

90

Celestial Bed

"The inspiration for celestial bed came from my desire to have storage compartments near my bed that would conceal the clutter that surrounds my sleeping area. The astrological side of the design reflects my love for celestial bodies.

The full-sized bed is composed of six species of wood – padauk, purpleheart, yellowheart, ash, Brazilian cherry, and maple – and accented with copper hardware.

Solid padauk rails connect the four cases/posts. The side rails are bolted into the cases of the headboard and footboard and angle iron is mounted on both to support the box spring and mattress.

The sides of the curved cases are layered 1/4" Baltic birch plywood vacuum-pressed and faced with padauk veneer. The cases of the foot board are shelving units fronted with padauk-veneered doors, while the headboard cases each contain five drawers. The contrasting drawer fronts are made from solid purpleheart, yellowheart and padauk. Below the drawers is a small veneered door which opens to reveal the lower part of the case.

Two arches constructed from nine laminated and half-lapped strips, join the cases of the headboard and footboard. The inset sun is made of solid yellowheart and Brazilian cherry, secured with polished copper rods. The footboard contains a solid purpleheart moon with an adjoining maple star."

– Katelyn Ander

Honorable Mention

Joshua Dale Peck • Cedar Ridge High School

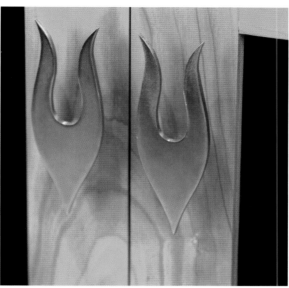
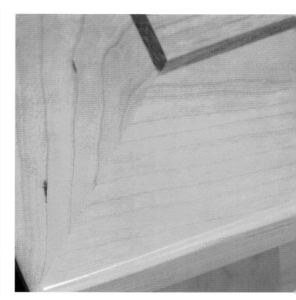

Entertainment Center

"My love for hot rods, muscle cars, and watching Norm Abrams with my father when I was little, as well as my specialty of drawing flames all came together – and I ended up with a modern entertainment center.

This entertainment center contains three units. The large unit holds stereo components and amplifiers. The two smaller units house the speakers. The large unit is 33" tall by 38" wide by 23" deep. The smaller cabinets are 27" tall by 20" wide by 17" deep. The cabinets are constructed from 3/4" cherry plywood, with the exposed plies edged with cherry veneer. The tops are 3/4" plywood with a 7/8" solid cherry border and a solid 1/4" by 1/4" padauk stripe inlaid between the solid wood and the plywood.

The base mold is a flame-inspired shape that resembles those on hotrods and ogee molding. The doors are solid cherry with dual rabbets to accept the padauk flame panels, and tinted glass in the large unit and speaker grill cloth in the smaller units. The hinges are based on the 32mm standard. The door stops are fluid filled for smooth operation. The door pulls are made from 3/16" stainless steel. The pulls were CNC laser cut and polished."

– Joshua Dale Peck

Finalist • Creative • Casework/Cabinets

Emory Luth • Shiloh High School

Cerca del Soñador

"This project was designed with function in mind. I wanted a bed design that could be used in different sizes as my lifestyle changed. It is a model of versatility because it will expand as the consumer's needs change. This design is unique in that it is expandable from a full to a California king size headboard in less than a minute using no tools. This versatility is accomplished through the use of slides that are mounted on the backside of the headboard. These slides not only make expansion possible, but also keep the star mounted perfectly in the center at all times.

Conventional woodworking processes were enhanced through the use of computer controlled machinery. The star and the two sides of the headboard were designed in AutoCAD, transferred to Mastercam and cut out on the Thermwood CNC machine. The star and trim were crafted from solid maple. The veneered surface of the headboard is Honduras mahogany laid in a diamond pattern and then stained with red mahogany."

— Emory Luth

Ryan Steffler • Torrance High School

Inlaid Clock

"This project is an inlaid clock and is made of cherry and purpleheart. The inlaid hour markers are made of pieces of purpleheart. The outer field pieces are made of cherry, using the grain to define the circular shape. A 1/16" band of purpleheart makes a circle around the centerpieces of the clock. Four pieces of cherry make up the circular centerpiece, with the grain going out from the center for a unique look.

I used the lathe to shape the 45-degree angles on the side and base of the clock. The same method of inlaid pieces of purpleheart was used on the base. The field pieces on the base were hand crafted to fit in. A motorized quartz movement was chiseled to fit in the back of the clock, along with an hour hand, a minute hand and a second hand. A felt piece on the bottom of the base gives it a smooth look. A polyurethane varnish finish gives the clock a beautiful gloss. All the pieces were custom designed and handcrafted."

– Ryan Steffler

Laura Williamson • Cedar Ridge High School

Oval Walnut Vanity

"I started this project by sketching several ideas. I fell in love with this one with its rich colors and random swirls of walnut. This traditional oval vanity blends air-dried, solid walnut and walnut burl veneer.

The initial oval around which this entire project was constructed, was cut at West Durham Lumber Company on a large CNC router, according to a pattern I designed on a computerized drafting program. The top was built by fitting solid walnut borders around three pieces of MDF and then veneered in a four-way book match. The center section, attached with two brass barrel hinges, lifts to reveal a console storage area and a mirror.

The curved panels and drawer fronts were constructed by bending six sheets of 1/8" Italian poplar over individually built forms and vacuum pressing. The drawers are traditional construction, featuring dovetails and three-sided, friction fit beveled cedar bottoms. I made a jig to cut the dovetails as they each fit the front panels at different angles.

The cabriole legs were handshaped of solid walnut, as were the curved wings that join them. These wings were especially difficult to cut and fit to the exact angle at which each leg sits, and it took several practice pairs to get them right."

– Laura Williamson

Honorable Mention

• Traditional • Casework/Cabinets

Ruslan Dorokhov • David Douglas High School

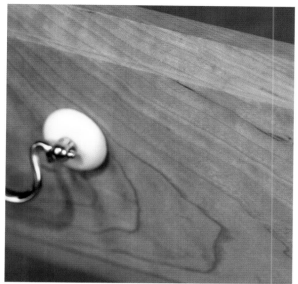

5-Drawer Cherry Dresser

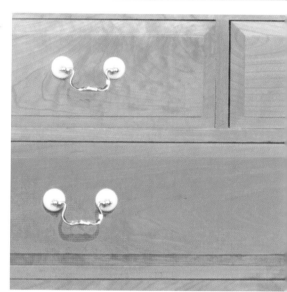

"My project is a five-drawer cherry dresser. I selected this project because I liked the look of the frame and panel construction, and chose cherry as I liked the look of natural finish on the wood. I liked the detail of the chamfer on the inside and outside of the stiles and the inside chamfer on the rails. I used stub mortise and tenons for the joinery and chose machine cut half-blind dovetails for the drawers because I wanted to learn the process. I was drawn to the 3" brass bail pulls which give the project a classic look.

One of the problems I faced was with the groove for the panel. I did not know that 1/4" plywood was not exactly 1/4". I set up a 1/4" dado, which made the groove too big for the plywood panel. I made filler strips and redid the groove with a single blade on the tablesaw with two passes. This worked out perfectly.

This project was interesting and a great challenge because it required making a lot of special set ups. Also, I had to make some jigs in order to give it the details I wanted. The chamfer jig that created the classic look was simple but it did a great job."

– Ruslan Dorokhov

Thomas Walter Tuck III • Cedar Ridge High School

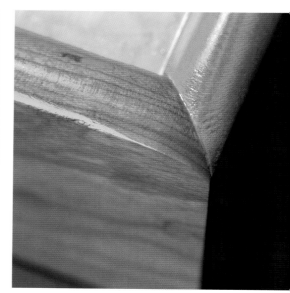

Bruno – Blanket Chest

"My inspiration came from an old World War II trunk brought back from Germany by my grandfather. The family has used the trunk for years and it has great sentimental value. I wanted to have another chest like it for my family one day. My design was taken from that military trunk and applied to an everyday blanket chest for storing blankets, quilts or pillows.

Bruno is a symmetrical design that was built the same from left to right, from side to side. A symmetrical design seemed necessary and pleasing to the eye, therefore it was constructed this way using AutoCAD.

In the production of Bruno, several complicated yet rewarding woodworking processes took place. The panels of the blanket chest were completed using cope and style cuts with a shaper. The uniquely curved top was completed using bent lamination and a vacuum press, with a form providing a foundation. The top was constructed with three layers of bending plywood and two layers of veneer, bird's-eye maple and cherry.

For the final detail, I added a cedar lining to protect against moth holes and replace a mothball smell with the pleasant distinct smell of cedar. This allows you to confidently store blankets over summer, knowing they will be kept in good shape."

— Thomas Walter Tuck III

Finalist • Traditional • Casework/Cabinets

Taylor Craig • Shiloh High School

Lion's Den

"I started the design process for my project by looking on the internet for existing centers. After looking at what was on the market, I drew my own entertainment center design in AutoCAD.

I used 2.5 face frame material for the frame of the carcase. The frame was joined together by pocket hole screws. All the plywood pieces for the carcase were presanded and refinished before assembling which was accomplished using 3/8" deep by 3/4" wide dadoes. The frame and carcase went together with a simple rabbet and groove joint. Once the basic shell was done, I flush-trimmed the frame edges to the cabinets sides.

I purchased the crown and rope moulding and ripped the rope moulding in half and glued it to the crown. The crown was applied to the cabinet top by building a substructure so the crown moulding was attached at the bottom and the top. I then turned my attention to the base moulding which was made from 3 separate pieces. The project was touched up, sanded, stained and finished. The doors were outsourced to Riverside Door Co. in Chesterville, IL. Smoked glass was installed in the doors and the doors were attached to the project. Lastly, the doors were leveled, and the magnetic catches and lion imprint pulls installed."

– Taylor Craig

105

Aaron L. Burns • Cedar Ridge High School

Weightless Mammoth

"Weightless Mammoth is a walnut china cabinet. The name Weightless Mammoth was derived from the floating appearance that the 33" high solid cabriolet legs give to the piece. The cabinet is 91" tall, 62 1/2" long, and 14 1/2" deep, with walnut-framed lipped glass doors with 3/8"-offset hinges and two adjustable shelves. The back, made of solid sappy worm holey walnut, is a solid panel with V-grooves to allow for expansion and contraction.

The idea for this piece came to me when my family added a dining room to the house. The room looked empty and a china cabinet seemed just the right thing to put in it. Most people are overwhelmed by the size of the piece; however its unique feature is that the top cabinet slides back, lifting up and off the base, allowing for easier transportation. The base is composed of mortise and tenoned legs attached to the aprons with a molded frame attached on the top. The molding on the base is the only thing that keeps the upper half of the piece in place.

I was pleased with the project as a whole but specifically the legs and the solid 'worm holey' back were an accomplishment alone. I have worked with wood for a little over three years."

— Aaron L. Burns

108

David Kibler • Shiloh High School

Star Watch

"I've always liked the antique look, and I like the old pie safes that were used to put the pies in to cool. I wanted my entertainment center to be a little different, but I based my design on the pie safe. I like the color of red oak so I used that and colonial maple, together with punched tin accents and black iron knobs and hinges.

The front of the cabinet is all face-frame stock. I used the pocket hole machine to make pocket holes to join the pieces. The doors are of hard red oak and I used the shaper to make the joint to join the parts together. The sides are regular plywood with red oak veneer on the inside and the outside. I screwed boards of red oak on purchased drawers to make the cabinet drawers.

I found the most difficult challenge was handcrafting the tin for the doors. Now that it is done, I am most pleased about the tinwork. I bought blank pieces of tin, designed the patterns, and hand-punched each tin with an awl."

–David Kibler

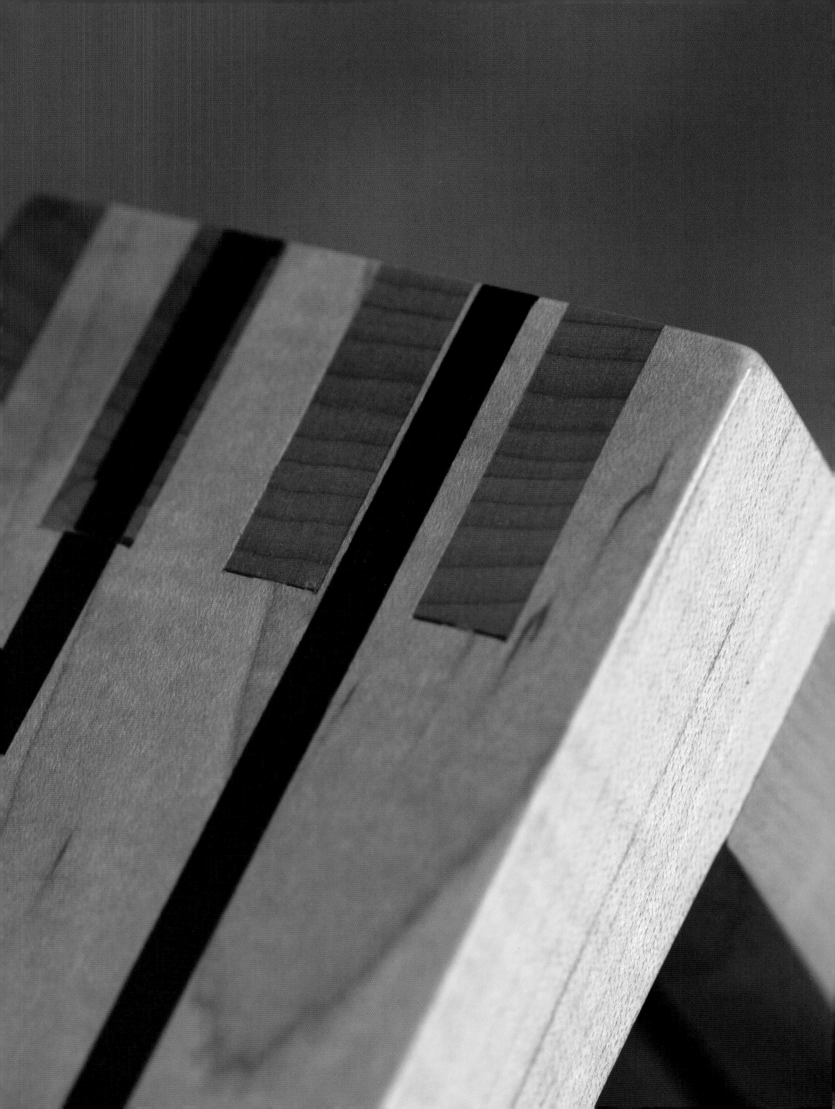

High School

Tables

Creative

Ashley Nichole Hilton, Cedar Ridge High School ....Dinner Table

Gray Burton, Cedar Ridge High School ....Kaleidoscope Coffee Table

Jens MacAller, Cedar Ridge High School ....W Table

Laura Williamson, Cedar Ridge High School ......Pentagon Display Table

Thomas Walter Tuck III, Cedar Ridge High School............X-treme Table

Wes Wegner, David Douglas High School ....Music Stand

Traditional

Michael S. Hoff, David Douglas High School ....Drop-Leaf Table

Paul Wilson, Shiloh High School ....Dubinater

First Place • Creative • Tables

Ashley Nichole Hilton • Cedar Ridge High School

Dinner Table

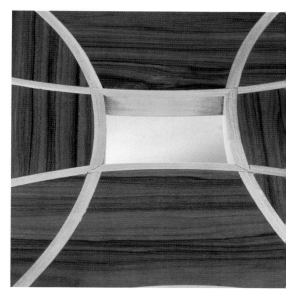

"Wanting to make something both traditional and beautiful for my future home was how my inspiration was first sparked. The most difficult challenge was getting the joints in the base to fit together perfectly and the seams of the 12-piece circular top to come together.

Multiple parts can multiply mistakes, and with a 12-piece pie slice table there is no room for error. With the help of a local company, (J&E Sketch Face Veneers, High Point NC), I was able to make all the pieces fit beautifully. J&E allowed me to come into their workplace and helped me learn to use their veneer cutter, which allowed all 12 pieces of veneer to be cut at once to assure a perfect fit. After the pieces were cut, I slip matched the veneer and taped the seams with gum tape, then used the heat press at J&E to glue the veneer to the MDF core.

The base of the dinner table is influenced by curves, yet is a different style from the top. It is constructed of four identical curved rosewood parts with half-lap joints. Strips of 1/8" inch maple were used for the inlay and glued to the outside edge of the base to accent the curves."

— Ashley Nichole Hilton

113

Honorable • Creative • Tables
Mention

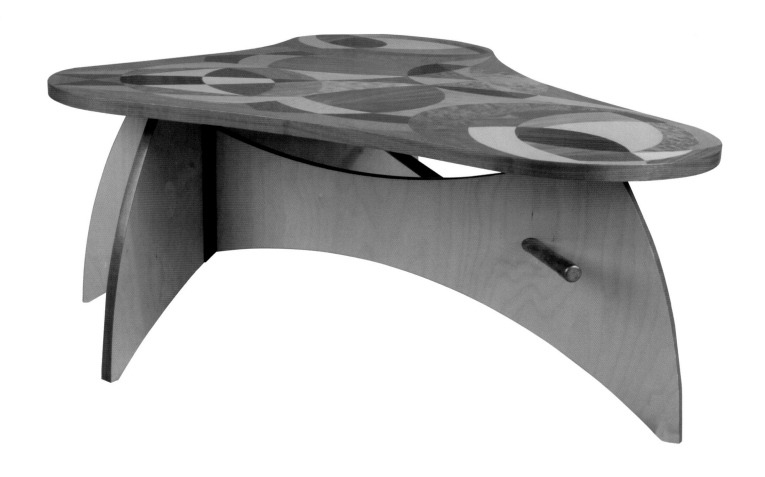

Gray Burton • Cedar Ridge High School

Kaleidoscope Coffee Table

"Creating from recycled pieces and making them interesting and useful is my inspiration. When I saw a pile of scrap veneer, I thought it looked like a kaleidoscope. A piece of found copper piping fit perfect with my design. I sketched out my idea and shared it with my instructor who said, "That's a haircut I don't want to get.""

This ready-to-assemble table measuring 16 1/2" high by 50" wide by 30 1/2" deep, is constructed from 20 different species of wood veneers. These handcut pieces coalesce in a flowing design that intertwines three circles on each end of the triangle. Walnut edgebanding was used around the perimeter of the tabletop.

The Baltic birch plywood base includes two flat legs that can be taken apart. To hide the joint where these two legs can be assembled, walnut trim is glued onto opposing sides of each leg. The leg edge arcs are cut from the same arc off a router trammel jig. The apron serves to attach the legs together, a copper pipe is used to connect the two. When the pipe is removed from the disassembled legs, the table can fit flat under a bed or in a closet. This table design is practical and ensures a sustainable use of materials."

– Gray Burton

Finalist • Creative • Tables

Jens MacAller • Cedar Ridge High School

W Table

"This creative coffee table (19" by 48" by 30") features two W-shaped legs with a shelf sitting on the middle point of the W. The legs are connected to the top by mortise and tenons. The W-shaped legs are each four pieces of solid maple finger joined at the desired angles. The top and bottom surfaces on each of the four leg parts feature two black inlaid stripes. Particleboard edged with solid maple makes up both the shelf and tabletop. The top and shelf are veneered with book matched quilted maple and backer grade maple, then pressed in a vacuum bag.

I liked the unusual shapes created by the joining legs and decided to add a cut window to the table. The window allows the viewer to see the detail of the legs and the unusual shapes from different angles."

– Jens MacAller

117

Finalist • Creative • Tables

Laura Williamson • Cedar Ridge High School

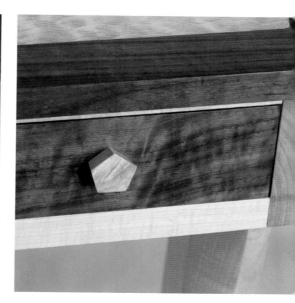

Pentagon Display Table

"I wanted to create a table that was small and delicate, yet sturdy and practical. My inspiration for the pentagon came from my love of geometry. I chose maple and walnut because they are rich and full of color. I love the way the walnut waves and looks like it wants to come alive.

The contrasting maple and walnut used in the construction of this table create a sleek and sophisticated, modern look. The sides of the pentagonal case are joined together by angled dovetails; I created a jig that allowed me to cut them on the bandsaw. I had to do a lot of hand work to clean up the cuts and make them fit perfectly. The front displays a walnut drawer and a small, pentagonal maple drawer pull. It took a couple of tries to get this piece just right.

The five curved and tapered legs on this piece were profile shaped with a flush-trim bit; they are secured into the dovetailed joints of the case. The pentagon tabletop features a walnut border surrounding a quilted maple veneer field. The border was cut and fit around the MDF center piece using a chopsaw.

This table can be used as a bedside table, a plant stand, a display table, or simply as a piece of art."

— Laura Williamson

Thomas Walter Tuck III • Cedar Ridge High School

X-treme Table

"Constructed of walnut and oak, this X-treme table is definitely one of a kind. It was designed out of pure imagination and uniqueness, made to serve no real purpose other than to look unusual and unlike any table seen before. Yet it also serves as a nice entryway and conversation piece.

The drawer of the table is ideal for storing things such as keys, gloves or small umbrella, serving all needs of an entryway table. The small storage space located just below the drawer is an open space where a purse or a few pieces of mail could go so they would be easily accessible on the way out the door.

In creating this table, there were a lot of difficult cuts and joinery. The legs of this table are complemented nicely with the X-top made of oak with a walnut inlay. The top is raised to stray away from a conventional flat tabletop surface. The raised inlay strips give the top a three-dimensional look and cause you to take a second glance. Glass was added to the surface of the table for protection of the fine woods and to create a display surface."

— Thomas Walter Tuck III

Wes Wegner • David Douglas High School

Music Stand

"This project's function is to hold sheet music while keeping a majestic look. I used the magnificent woods of black walnut and purpleheart on the desk to imitate blue ink on black lines, just like a composer would create. I designed the top to resemble the feel of flowing music. As the lines move to the right they break parallel form, just as musical tone follows no restrictions. The notes and time signatures were carefully cut with a scrollsaw and give the stand a connection with its purpose. All notes and lines were inlaid by hand. I capped the top of the two back legs with domed purpleheart to establish the desk and the stand as one piece. The handmade brass knob adds a shimmering brass effect to the stand.

There is approximately 30" between each leg of the tripod base, and the stand reaches 5' tall. The legs of this project are made of 1/8" laminated strips bent over a form. The concave front and angled back give a remarkable design. The 60-degree angled biscuit joints that join the legs together proved to be the hardest part to execute. It was difficult to perfect the joint. The quality of this project is in its impeccable design and will bring out the artistic ability of any musician."

– Wes Wegner

First Place • Traditional • Tables

Michael S. Hoff • David Douglas High School

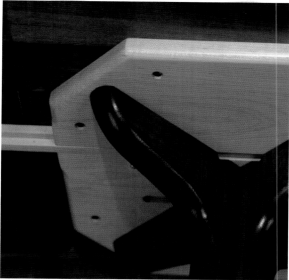

Drop-Leaf Table

"I built a contemporary occasional drop-leaf table. My inspiration for this table came from a picture in a *Rockler* catalog of a table built by Sam Maloof. When I saw the picture, I fell in love with the curves and the design of the drop leaf-table hinge. I was worried that I would break copyright laws, so I sought and received permission from Sam Maloof before building my table.

I built the table out of aged black walnut that had been sitting in a barn for many years and donated to the school. When I received it, I immediately knew it would be good for this project because of the character in the wood. I struggled with designing the legs because of the knee that was in them. All I had to go by was the picture. Once I had designed the curve of the legs, I made a template to follow. I also made a template for the top but still ran into problems and had to redesign it.

I applied a great finish that is made by Sam Maloof. This was a fun and challenging project. I hope I did justice to my dream and to Sam Maloof's craftsmanship."

— Michael S. Hoff

125

Finalist • Traditional • Tables

Paul Wilson • Shiloh High School

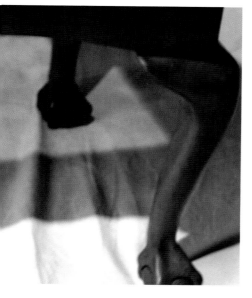

Dubinater

"I built a coffee table with tinted glass in the middle, made of cherry and stained a dark walnut. It is 48" long by 21" wide by 18" tall. The provincial contour around the top has a profiled edge. The skirt pieces follow the same design as the top piece, only without the profiled edge.

Four corner pieces with bolt hangars hold the legs to the table and add rigidity to the table's construction. They are all cut at 45 degree angles on each side. They have a groove cut in them so the screws are at 90 degrees to the skirt. I stained and sprayed these four pieces because they can be seen through the glass. They were the hardest things to make on the table.

This project combines traditional tools with a CNC router. The top was designed with Mastercam. I also created the tool paths and G&M for assembly purposes. The table is held together by screws, which allow the table to be disassembled. This design makes for a smaller shipping container. It can be sold unfinished and unassembled, or finished and assembled. The legs were outsourced to Adams Wood Products, Morristown, TN. This allows for a variety of leg choices and thus more table designs."

– Paul Wilson

High School

Upholstery

Traditional

Ashley Nichole Hilton, Cedar Ridge High School............Chaise Lounge

First Place • Traditional • Upholstery

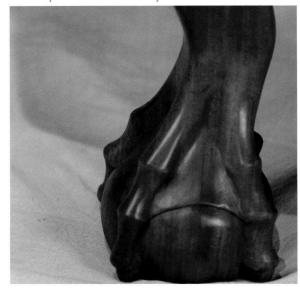

Ashley Nichole Hilton • Cedar Ridge High School

Chaise Lounge

"The chaise lounge features cabriole legs with hand carved ball and claw feet. The poplar frame is attached to the legs by mortise and tenons. For support there are three poplar stretchers spaced along the frame. The arm of the lounge is made from poplar with sapele veneer. The frame was formed by bending plywood and then veneer. The arm is bolted onto the frame and to the back with T-nuts. The back is made from 8/4 sapele. The pattern of the grain on the back is from book matching two boards. There are spring coils along the frame for support and a mixture of high and low-density foam beneath the chenille fabric for cushioning.

The Chaise Lounge was inspired by a modern chaise. However, as my taste leans towards more traditional styles, I kept the basic shape of one armrest and a curved back, but decided to use ball and claw feet and dark wood. I practiced carving ball and claw feet on poplar before construction. I researched different styles of feet from different time periods. Then when I began carving, I used the basic style and form and added a little of my own style. A router jig was used on the lathe to carve the ball of the leg."

— Ashley Nichole Hilton

High School

Special Theme

Creative

First Place • Creative • Special Theme

Jens MacAller • Cedar Ridge High School

Executive Desk

"My need for a desk was my initial inspiration. I wanted something nice and also unique. The majestic executive desk features two file drawers, a writing tablet and four different storage drawers.

The desk (31.5" by 68" by 35") is assembled from three pieces: the top, and the left and right drawer cases. The drawer cases are constructed by biscuiting the veneered side panels into the rabbet in the tapered bubinga posts. Each drawer case is curved back and away from the sitting space to match the curve of the desktop. Bent laminations make up the curved drawer fronts. The shallow pencil drawer has a solid maple front with recesses for small supplies. Book-matched waterfall bubinga was used for the desktop and writing tablet. The desktop is constructed of a veneered and backed MDF panel, honeycomb core, 1/4" plywood, and covered with a layer of dark paper backer.

A honeycomb core keeps the desktop to a minimal weight without giving up structural integrity. The drawer pulls are handmade and individually fit to each drawer. The trick was to find a good way to attach the drawer fronts to the odd-shaped drawer boxes. Oversized holes and drawer front screws allowed for slight adjustments while pocket screws locked the front in place once properly positioned."

— Jens MacAller

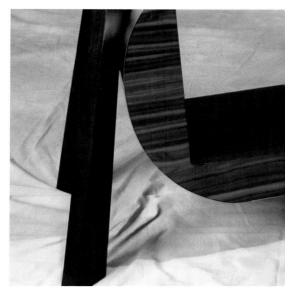

Floating Book/
Display Case

"Inspired by the great designs and simple lines of pioneers such as Charles and Ray Eames, this sculptural piece, measuring 82" high by 52" wide by 15 1/2" deep, was designed to house books and other items for display. Constructed of santos rosewood veneer, sheet stainless steel, birch plywood and painted poplar, the three display cylinders appear to be floating, suspended between two large, black-lacquer posts on either side.

Beginning as three rectangular boxes constructed from plywood, a pattern for the oval faces was made for each box. Using a flush-trim router bit, the faces of the boxes were routed to size. The rosewood veneer was seamed to fit each face, and urea formaldehyde glue was used to attach the veneer to the faces in a vacuum press. Four posts constructed from 8/4 poplar were drawn from a custom pattern, jig-sawed out, and flush-trim routed. The veneer was routed to fit the faces and then the boxes. The posts and insides were painted black and all was given a lacquer finish. The ovals were wrapped with stainless steel and the assembly holes drilled. Once assembled, this sculpture becomes art on display instead of just the art it is intended to house."

— Gray Burton

Index of Schools

High Schools

Cedar Ridge High School's Furniture and Cabinetmaking program seeks to get the students excited about the art of woodworking, ground them in the basics and encourage them to continue to discover the vast opportunities in the world of wood. Courses cover beginning woodworking to advanced studies over four years. Students are prepared for entry-level employment in wood-related fields or continuing education at the postsecondary level.

Topics covered start with wood properties and traditional green woodworking practices and move into basic machine woodworking practices. Advanced classes are taught through individualized projects designed by the students and reinforce the principals of woodworking, and introduce advanced machining practices, veneering, marquetry, inlay, vacuum pressing, bent laminations, hardware applications, finishing, carving, sharpening, tool maintenance, furniture design, use of innovative wood products and employment opportunities. Students are encouraged to participate in a regional trade show and national design contests. Cedar Ridge High is a WoodLINKS USA school.

Cedar Ridge High School
1125 New Grady Brown School Road
Hillsborough, North Carolina 27278
(919) 245-4000
www.orange.k12.nc.us/crhs
Students' instructor: Keith Yow

The motto at David Douglas High School is "A Place Where Connections are Made." The Wood Manufacturing Technology program lives up to this motto as the students connect the theory they learn in the academic world and the practical skills they learn in the vocational world. Louis L'Amour makes the connection between the muscle and the mind when he states:

> "There is a knowledge in the muscles of a workman that goes beyond the mind, a skill that lies in the flesh and the fiber, and my hands and heart held a love for the wood, the good wood whose fresh chips fell cleanly to the left and the right."

Connections are also made as we offer a four year program that provides students not only with specific woodworking skills but also includes appreciation of the environment. We give the students work experience opportunities through job shadows and internships with wood working companies in our community. A large percentage of our students are ready for entry-level job positions and/or choose to continue their wood working education. David Douglas High is a WoodLINKS USA school.

David Douglas High School
1001 SE 135 Avenue
Portland, Oregon 97233
(503) 252-2900
http://ddhs.ddouglas.k12.or.us/
Students' instructor: Doug Ivey

The Industrial Technology program at Shiloh High School is based on the belief that the individual's security in the workforce is achieved through a foundation of practical education based on the knowledge and skills needed by businesses, industries and communities in our society. To that end, the program offers applied courses in AutoCAD, manufacturing, production and CAD/CAM, as well as numerous opportunities to work with businesses and homeowners in the area.

Students learn a variety of skills in the three manufacturing classes. The CAD/CAM class covers machine code and Mastercam generated code, as well as the basics of CNC machine operations. Students in the upper level of AutoCAD work on projects for the school district, local businesses and contractors, producing architectural drawings and shop drawings. Each year, students build custom kitchen cabinets for homeowners locally and around the state, allowing them to experience many challenges and pressures any company would face, including material handling, safety issues, quality control, time management, precise measurement, preparation processes, combination processes, coating technology, customer service, etc. Shiloh High School is a WoodLINKS USA school.

Shiloh High School
21751 North 575 Street
Hume, Illinois 61932-9707
(217) 887-2364
www.shiloh.k12.il.us
Students' instructor: Mark Smith

Index of Schools

Torrance High School
2200 West Carson Street
Torrance, California 90501
(310) 533-4396
www.torrancehigh.com
Students' instructor: Abe Rivera

The Wood Technology program in the Applied Technology department is a two-tier program. Wood 1AB instruction covers safety, handtools, machine tools, material processes, measurement, calculation of materials, adhesives, abrasives, fasteners, jointery, project planning, project cost projection, and finishing materials and procedures. Students will construct a laminated cutting board, a jewelry box and a shaker table. Other projects of the student's choice may be made as time permits. The Wood 2AB program prerequisite is one year of Wood 1AB with a passing grade of C or better. This is an in-depth course of cabinetry, furniture construction techniques, advanced milling and machine operations in the preparation of field trade skills for furniture construction: advanced joinery, drawer construction, face framing, moulding, carcase construction, materials selection, project planning and cost estimation, fastener and hardware installation, and advanced finishing processes. Projects for the Wood 2AB class are an inlaid clock and a lamp project (lathe), a curio cabinet and a mini chest. We also have a third tier of independent study with an emphasis on professional career development.

Postsecondary Schools

Art Center College of Design
1700 Lida Street
Pasadena, California 91103-1999
(626) 396-2200
www.artcenter.edu/furniture
Students' instructor: David Mocarski

The Environmental Design degree program at the Art Center College of Design seeks to foster the appreciation and ability to recognize, enhance and create beauty and meaning in both built and non-built environments and experiences. Students research, practice and explore the full spectrum of environmental design in an experimental and creative atmosphere. Areas of study include furniture, lighting, film and theater sets, interiors, buildings, landscapes and urbanism, in addition to environmental art, environmental graphics, digital environments and more.

While furniture design is only one 14-week studio in the Environmental Design program, students are able to produce well-conceived and finished pieces due to comprehensive core studios focusing on design, design process and technical skills. Graduates pursue careers in areas such as set design for film and theater, production design for film, interior architecture, environmental graphics, lighting and exhibit design, experience design, digital/multimedia environments and theme park design.

Auburn University
237 Wallace Center
Auburn, Alabama 36849-5121
(334) 844-2364
www.auburn.edu/ind/
Students' instructor: Sang-Gyeun Ahn

The Industrial Design program at the Auburn University College of Architecture, Design and Construction offers undergraduates and graduate students a very broad-based experience in industrial design, encompassing multiple facets of consumer and specialty product design within a given cultural and economic context. The program includes a woodworking studio once a year as part of the senior level studio sequence. The required subjects cover computer software, rendering, materials and technology, photography, design methodology, portfolio, anthropometry, professional practice, design history and, of course, design studios every semester.

Completion of the bachelor's degree enables students to assume leadership roles in industries such as packaging, exhibition design, product design, graphic design, computer interface design, way finding, furniture design and all types of information delivery systems. The department has relationships with various industry organizations including Crate and Barrel, Inc., and participates in a number of exhibits and design competitions including the International Woodworking Fair (Design Emphasis).

The furniture design courses at Brigham Young University are taught within the Industrial Design program in the School of Technology. While a variety of materials are used in our furniture design courses, we offer three classes which include significant instruction in working and designing in wood. These courses include model making/prototype construction, beginning furniture design and advanced furniture design.

The primary goal within the Industrial Design program is to prepare leaders in the design profession in one of three areas of emphasis – Product Design, Transportation Design and Furniture design. Students complete courses in drawing (technical, perceptual and perspective), prototyping, presentation methods, computer modeling, history of products, form and shape development, etc. The four-year Industrial Design program includes 70 major-related semester credit hours and graduates earn a Bachelor of Fine Arts degree.

One of the best features of the BYU Industrial Design program is its close tie with industry. Many of the BFA studio projects are industry sponsored, and each student is required to complete an internship in a design-related enterprise in their area of emphasis. In addition, faculty members are energetic and passionate about the subject matter and committed to the success of the students. Our students have access to excellent studios/facilities housed within the School of Technology and the College of Engineering and Technology.

Brigham Young University
265 CTB
P.O. Box 24206
Provo, Utah 84602
(801) 422-6300
www.byu.edu
Students' instructor: Kip Christensen, Ph.D

The Cerritos College Department of Woodworking Manufacturing Technology (WMT) offers training on state of the art automated cabinetmaking equipment as well as traditional woodworking machinery and hand tools. Students have access to over twenty talented and dedicated faculty members as well as a comprehensive variety of machinery and supplies in the 30,000 square foot WMT facility, which operates seven days a week.

The program offerings include courses in Comprehensive Woodworking, Furniture Making and Manufacturing, Cabinetmaking and Manufacturing and Computer Operations for Woodworking. Many graduates of the program successfully enter the wood industry, as the WMT degree and certificate programs provide students with a complete background as well as the most current understanding of technology as it is applies to their area of choice. This is accomplished by blending classroom theory with hands on work experience. Special emphasis is placed on training for specific job skills in a safe and productive environment where craftsmanship is never sacrificed.

Cerritos College
11110 East Alondra Boulevard
Norwalk, California 90650
(562) 860-2451
www.cerritos.edu/wood
Students' instructors: John Nyquist, Tony Fortner, Tony Atherton

Index of Schools

Fullerton College
321 East Chapman Avenue
Fullerton, California 92632
(714) 992-7247
www.fullcoll.edu/
Students' instructor: Tim Harrison

The Fullerton College Wood Technology program within the Construction Technology Department seeks to produce good craftsmen and craftswomen who are well prepared to enter the workforce with a high level of skill and technical training. To that end, the department is aggressive in purchasing new equipment that uses modern technologies. In addition, the instructors have real-world experience and work to create a friendly, helpful environment in the woodshop to enhance learning.

We have a fundamentals class each semester so that students can gain the basic skills and safety instruction necessary to be successful in their intermediate and advanced classes. Those classes include furniture making, cabinetmaking, table and chair construction, 32mm cabinetmaking, woodcarving, tools and jigs and CAD (Cabnetware) to name a few. Students can take a prescribed sequence of courses leading to a vocational certificate in cabinetmaking, or a shorter sequence of courses leading to shorter specialist certificates in cabinetmaking, furniture making and woodcarving. Upon completion of any of these certificates, we expect our students to be prepared to enter the woodworking workforce at a well-paid level.

Georgia Institute of Technology, College of Architecture
247 4th Street
Atlanta, Georgia 30332-0155
(404) 894.3880
www.coa.gatech.edu/
Students' instructor: Alan Harp

The Georgia Institute of Technology offers a Certificate of Furniture Design and Manufacturing through the College of Architecture. The certificate is comprised of a choice of five classes covering the topics of furniture design, history, theory, CNC production, universal design and independent study. Participating students are typically from the Industrial Design or Architecture programs, and are entering their junior year or in the graduate program. The students are exposed to a wide array of theory and technology during the program as both practicing architects and designers teach the courses. The CNC course is conducted at the Advanced Wood Products Laboratory (AWPL), a research center of the College of Architecture. AWPL has a state of the art 13,000 square foot shop facility with several CNC manufacturing centers as well as traditional woodworking machinery.

Students who graduate with this certificate will also have a degree in Industrial Design or Architecture and can expect to be finding employment in a variety of design firms locally and nationally. Georgia Tech has a well-established intern and research program from which many students find their first job.

Jefferson Technical College
727 West Chestnut Street
Louisville, Kentucky 40203-2036
(502) 213-4242
www.jtc.kctcs.edu/
Students' instructor: Grant Gamble

The Wood Manufacturing Technology program at Jefferson Technical College has been offered since 1999 and is dedicated to providing an educated workforce for a large industry base in a two-state region. Students can earn one-year certifications in Furniture Manufacturing, Cabinetmaking Technology, and Millwork Technology; a two-year Wood Technologist diploma; or an associate degree in applied science in General Occupational and Technical Studies with an emphasis in Wood Manufacturing Technology.

Jefferson's state of the art facility represents approximately a half-million dollar investment by the college and Kentucky Wood Products Competitiveness Corp. The facilities not only allow students to work in shop while taking classes as part of a sponsorship or internship, but they also allow for instruction in hardwood processing, computer integrated panel processing and wood finishing. Jefferson's Wood Manufacturing Technology program also offers a national certification in spray painting for HVLP and other commercial spray-coating applications.

The college is part of the Jefferson Community & Technical College District, a 13,500-student, five-campus district that is part of the Kentucky Community & Technical College System.

With an annual enrollment of 2,000 students in over 50 different classes, the Palomar College Cabinet and Furniture Technology program offers the most comprehensive woodworking curriculum in the nation. Utilizing three fully equipped shops, our 5 full-time and 12 part-time instructors provide a breadth of courses and depth of expertise impossible to obtain in smaller programs.

Our courses range from Furniture Design to Timber Framing, and from Guitar Building to Production Cabinetmaking. Whether your goal is to build the skills to enrich your retirement or position yourself for a lifetime of satisfying work, we have the courses for you.

By the end of our program students will have had the opportunity to build everything from a hand-crafted clock to an elegant Sam Maloof rocking chair. All we ask is that our students stay as dedicated to mastering the technical skills of traditional and contemporary fine woodworking as we are to teaching them.

Palomar College
1140 West Mission Road
San Marcos, California 92069-1487
(760) 744-1150
www.palomar.edu/
Students' instructor: Craig Bradley

The Wood Technology program at Pittsburg State University is a national leader in preparing young men and women for rewarding managerial careers in the secondary wood products industry. The program features the highest quality instruction for a low cost to the student, as well as an outstanding new 270,000 square foot facility with state of the art equipment and technology.

Bachelor of Science in Wood Technology, and Associate of Arts degree programs are available. The comprehensive curriculum uses a hands-on approach that takes students from "the log to the finished products," with a broad base of technical knowledge and skills. Much of the coursework is production-based and blends classroom theory with real-world product and process engineering problems. Courses include Wood Science, Primary Wood Processing, Machine Woodworking, Production Techniques, Cabinets & Fixtures, Mill & Casework, Furniture Design, Software Applications, Computer Numerical Control, Finishing, Tool Technology, and Residential Construction. Students also may pursue one or more specializations in Wood Product Manufacturing, Finishing Technology or Residential Construction.

Pittsburg State University
1701 South Broadway
Pittsburg, Kansas 66762
(620) 235-4365
www.pittstate.edu/tech
Students' instructor: Lindy Thomsen

The Industrial Design Department seeks to educate students to identify and resolve design problems, both innovatively and with sensitivity to the social, physical and ecological environment. Students learn traditional values of industrial design and gain an in-depth understanding of visual and three-dimensional vocabulary. CAD and other digital media programs are taught using laptop computers that all students are required to purchase. In the studio, students progress from developmental drawings through three-dimensional mock-ups and models to working drawings and construction with manufacturing considerations. A number of elective courses in furniture design are offered as well.

There are numerous opportunities within the program for students to work with industry through internships and corporate-sponsored studio projects. Also, the department collaborates on projects with other school departments, in addition to working with other schools, including Harvard Business School and The Sloan School at MIT. Upon completion, students can enter the field of design at either an industrial or entrepreneurial level.

Rhode Island School of Design
Two College Street
Providence, Rhode Island 02903
(401) 454-6100
www.risd.edu/
Students' instructor: Seth Stem

143

Index of Schools

Rockingham Community College
P.O. Box 38
Wentworth, North Carolina 27375
(336) 342-4261
www.rcc.cc.nc.us
Students' instructor: David Kenealy

The Fine and Creative Woodworking curriculum prepares individuals to design and build high quality furniture and accessories. Students may choose to work in period styles, creative work, or both. This program provides an opportunity to expand skill level and creativity in building fine furniture.

The students will begin by developing a strong foundation in basic hand tool use and machining. Course work progresses to include study in finishing, turning, carving, jigs and fixtures, veneering, bending, equipment maintenance, principles of operating a business and more.

Graduates may earn an Associate degree, diploma, or certificate. This program concentrates on preparing graduates to establish a business of their own. In addition, graduates may find employment opportunities in high-end custom furniture shops or the furniture manufacturing industry.

Savannah College of Art and Design
P.O. Box 3146
Savannah, Georgia 31402-3146
(800) 869-7223
www.scad.edu/
Students' instructor: Richard Prisco

The Furniture Design Program focuses specifically on the objects society uses to organize and enhance living environments. The challenge of a furniture design student is to successfully balance aesthetic and conceptual concerns with emotional, intellectual and functional requirements.

The undergraduate furniture design program at the Savannah College of Art and Design emphasizes design methodology, fabrication skills and presentation techniques, allowing students to effectively communicate their concepts. The study of furniture and its related markets and the examination of cultural, conceptual, ecological and contemporary issues provide a context for student work.

Students in the graduate program gain an understanding of conceptual issues, a design methodology, critical analysis skills and advanced technical proficiency. Master of fine arts students express their design philosophy in a thesis and produce a comprehensive body of work for exhibition.

Furniture design is housed in the Gulfstream Center for Furniture and Industrial Design, a 40,000-square-foot state of the art facility. The program maintains one of the most extensive fabrication and prototyping facilities in the United States.

The main objective of the Selkirk College Fine Woodworking program is to ready students for employment or self-employment by developing flexible and readily portable skills. The introductory program is broad in scope and encourages students to strive for quality design, originality and enhanced workmanship skills to improve chances of success in the world of designing and making of fine wood objects.

The first year is a nine-month introductory program, which covers the process of designing, drafting, planning, costing, constructing, documenting and marketing of fine wood products. There are four benches made available for students who desire to come back for a second year of study. The focus for this specialty year is on independent study. Each student sets out their goals for the year and then works on achieving them. In the Selkirk College Fine Woodwork, our standards and expectations for the students are set very high and it is amazing what can happen in the span of nine months.

Selkirk College
Silver King Campus
2001 Silver King Rd
Nelson, British Columbia V1L 1C8
Canada
(250) 352-6601
www.selkirk.ca
Students' instructor: Michael Grace

The Industrial Design Program (ID) at Western Michigan University incorporates the woodworking and furniture design courses. The mission of ID is to provide a dynamic learning environment promoting discovery, creativity and innovation for the education of Industrial Designers who can cross functional boundaries to other professions and can become leaders in industry and the community. We develop competent and responsible professional designers who are focused and dedicated to excellence in design.

We want our program to be known as a leader in industrial design education addressing professional, social and global needs. Graduates are fully prepared for the global market and for interaction and teamwork in the business environment. We will always evolve to meet changing social and technological developments to enrich the learning experience of our students and to maintain a relevant curriculum to promote the business value of design.

The spacious and well equipped ID studios promote innovations and creativity in the development of models, furniture and other projects. Focused areas of learning are in 2D and 3D Visualization, Concept Development, User Centered Design, Computer Design Skills, Engineering, Manufacturing Processes, New Materials, Technologies and Business Objectives.

The ID students enjoy cooperation with the neighboring industrial companies throughout the sponsored projects and internships. Upon graduation students can attain responsible design positions in the global market.

Western Michigan University
1903 West Michigan Avenue
Kalamazoo, Michigan 49008
(269) 387-3530
www.wmich.edu/
Students' instructor: Roman Rabiej, PhD.

Index of Students

WoodLINKS USA

WoodLINKS
USA

An Industry
Education Partnership

A True Partnership Between Industry and Education

WoodLINKS USA is successfully revitalizing high school woodworking programs across the country by connecting high schools with industry partners. The program, which originated in Canada, grew out of a need in the wood industry for skilled, entry-level workers. As the industry changed and became more technologically advanced, it was apparent that high school wood shop training was not. Most high schools throughout the country had either abandoned "old wood shop programs" altogether or were using antiquated equipment. Furthermore, teachers, counselors, students and parents had little or no idea of the career opportunities offered by wood product manufacturers.

WoodLINKS USA was launched in 2000 by enterprising U.S industry leaders who were familiar with WoodLINKS Canada and sought to establish a similar program in the United States. Through donations and support from trade associations, industry and a few enthusiastic teachers, the dream became a reality. Four initial pilot programs have grown to over forty sites delivering the WoodLINKS program.

Through WoodLINKS USA, wood industries link up with a public education program – high school or technical school – to work together in creating and delivering a wood manufacturing program that meets the needs of the local wood industry profile.

Students are taught a standardized skill set with some coursework placing emphasis on the types of wood business in the school's geographic area. WoodLINKS provides assistance to schools in how to connect to their local industry sources and build a strong wood education program in the school – one that industry directly benefits from.

The goal of WoodLINKS USA is to certify high school students to a National Industry Standard for the wood industry. In addition to producing entry-level skilled workers, many students go on to college or university wood manufacturing programs to become teachers or future managers and leaders in the industry.

The supporting local industries play a "big brother" leadership role in helping schools, teachers and students understand and appreciate the career opportunities that are offered and the technologies that are used in producing their wood products. Some also provide internships for the students. AWFS® has initiated a scholarship program specifically for graduates of the WoodLINKS USA program.

Fresh Wood

Order more copies of **Fresh Wood** and support woodworking education – 40% of the net proceeds are donated to WoodLINKS USA.

To Order **Fresh Wood** Visit: www.mitrapublishing.com

Mitra Publishing Group
    255 No. Lima St. Suite 6
    Sierra Madre, CA 91024
    Email: info@mitrapublishing.com

For orders of 25 or more: group pricing is available and company logos and names can be imprinted on the book jacket. Call (626) 836-3300 or email for information.